12 C

HYPNOSIS SESSIONS TO PREPARE HUMANITY FOR ASCENSION

THE DISCOURSE

JILL COLE & ALBA WEINMAN

The Discourse

PUBLISHER
Jill Cole
P.O. Box 816
Wanaka 9343
Central Otago
South Island
New Zealand

ISBN 978-0-473-56588-6 (paperback)
ISBN 978-0-473-56587-9 (softcover – POD Amazon)
ISBN 978-0-473-56589-3 (Kindle)

Publishing services supplied by:
PublishMe, New Plymouth, New Zealand.
www.publishme.co.nz

CONTENTS

FOREWORD

ALBA WEINMAN

My participation in The Discourse began on a cold, windy evening in Wellington, New Zealand on 9 September 2017. I had scheduled a few hypnosis sessions while I was there, and Jill was my last client.

My first impression of Jill Cole was one of a beautiful, classy businesswoman. She had flown in from Wanaka, a small ski village on the South Island, and shared a writing that had been given to her by her guides.

The part that caught my attention said:

> "Like attracts like. It is timely that you meet THE AMERICAN. This is work that needs to be undertaken in its truest form, for as thou serves self, thou serves others with this work, as does THE AMERICAN.
>
> "Her work is pure, and we have said that we wish for you to be such a vessel, crystalline of structure and clean to be seen through, without fault or flaws, for what is it that we speak, but of a cellular structure and nature.

> “We speak of grounding and to be grounded, but you ground not; you float and dither, but fear not, for you are not alone.
>
> “We spoke to you before of bringing to you the ones to help you with your work.
>
> “We spoke of your work crossing the seas; the work has come to you from across the sea and as such you will return to it.
>
> “There is much to be done, many to meet, many to assist in these testing times ahead. THE AMERICAN has a knowing and, as such, it is your knowing, for it is within you as such as it is within her.”

Since I also connect with my Higher Self through automatic writing, I understood that our guides had brought us together, and this meeting was not by chance.

During her session (video # 166: Ambassador from the Inter-galactic Federation of Light) she was told about *The Discourse*, but I did not know how I would be working with Jill in the future because I lived so far away.

On 16 January 2019, Jill invited me to come back to New Zealand to do a Gathering in Wanaka and suggested that I ask my colleague, Antonio Sangio, to come and do an Introspective Hypnosis class.

Jill was able to gather enough participants for both events and helped us find the venue.

We held both events in September 2019 after I facilitated another hypnosis session for Jill (video # 352: The Light Traveler and the Ascension).

The subject of The Discourse came up again, and I was getting the feeling that her guides were not going to give up on this idea.

In February 2020, I saw Jill again, along with many of the students from our Wanaka Introspective Hypnosis class, who had signed up for a Gathering and a tour that Antonio Sangio had arranged in Peru.

During that week, we traveled and bonded with our soul family and our bodies received new photons and energy patterns.

Most of us felt that we tapped into psychic and metaphysical abilities that we had not had before. After we left Peru, we came home to a different world facing the Covid-19 pandemic, and the shutdown of borders and travel.

All travel plans for 2020 were cancelled and my hypnosis sessions were facilitated over Zoom.

In June 2020, I facilitated the third hypnosis session for Jill online.

Her guides gave her topics or questions for me to ask during that session and both the guides and I would expand to other topics.

We were told that this was the beginning of *The Discourse*, which would have a total of twelve sessions.

At first, Jill and I both thought that we would just be writing the book but after session # 3 (video # 403 The Awakening) the guides told us to publish the videos on YouTube.

The experience has been profound for me and I feel honored to have been the one conversing with these guides through Jill and learning so much from them. This is a gift of love that we give to the world.

JILL COLE

My guides told me Alba would be hypnotising me twelve times and they would channel the questions and messages through me. You can view ten of the chapters on Alba's YouTube channel.

Session # 403 (chapter three) was profound. James, Jesus's brother, made his first appearance. It was intense. There is so much more to be shared with you all, but at least this is a start to a much bigger conversation. Let The Discourse begin.

ABOUT JILL COLE

JILL COLE – Website: www.jillcole.org

International hypnotherapist, author, medium, public speaker and energy healer.

Jill channels Jesus, his brother James, and two Archangels (Michael and Uriel), as well as Dominus and Aurelius, who have been with her for many years, and Urka, her soul manager. Simon the disciple made a brief appearance just for this book.

Jill was born in South Africa and moved to New Zealand in 1987 with her Kiwi husband. They live in Wanaka and have two adult sons living in Australia.

ABOUT ALBA WEINMAN

ALBA WEINMAN, CCHt – albaweinman.com

Hypnotherapist, author, Spiritual Life Coach

Alba began her hypnosis career by learning the Quantum Healing Hypnosis Technique (QHHT®) from Dolores Cannon, a world-renowned hypnotherapist and author specialising in past life regression.

She was then mentored by Aurelio Mejia, a Colombian hypnotherapist, who developed *La Hipnosis Introspectiva* (Introspective Hypnosis), a method that combines hypnosis with dynamics of forgiveness and spirituality to achieve behavioural changes and relief in the client.

Alba was certified as a clinical and transpersonal hypnotherapist by the Institute of Interpersonal Hypnotherapy, a state-licensed hypnotherapy school in Florida.

She calls her hypnosis method The Spiritual Journey of

Forgiveness™, reminding people of the awesome, creative, and transformative power of our Creator within us.

Through her YouTube channel, Alba shares her clients' amazing experiences with people around the world who are on the path of spiritual awakening.

These hypnosis sessions not only benefit Alba's clients but also affect the viewers who watch her videos.

CHAPTER ONE

CREATION

In this hypnosis session Jill tells us that we have the ability to manipulate our body's energy to create wellness. We learn about volunteers, ascension, what a soul family is, and who or what we actually are.

A: You enter an ancient sacred doorway to a chamber of secrets that you are privileged to know about. Begin now by entering and going inside, and as you do, you will notice the walls and how they feel. How do the walls feel to you?

J: *They are different, some are very smooth, like marble, just like smooth stone. Then it changes to writing, so it's writing and it's rough.*

A: As you touch the writings on this wall, you will be able to connect to the lifetime in which you recognise this writing. Transport yourself now into that time period. Allow yourself to touch the wall and begin to receive the knowledge from this place. What is the message that the writing tells you about today?

J: *I get two names; the first name is Uriel and the second name is Uranus.*

A: Are these beings?

J: *Uriel is a being; Uranus is a destination.*

A: Very good, is this where you will be going today?

J: *Uriel is laughing. He said he is going on what is called "a magical mystery tour" or "a tiki tour." He says, "Let's go globetrotting."*

A: I would like you to go ahead and tell me what he is doing and where you are going.

J: *He wants to show us the layout of the planets and the interconnection between them all.*

A: All right. Are these the planets around our sun?

J: *Yes, he says it's how it affects our solar system.*

A: Wonderful. So, describe to me everything that you experience.

J: *I have an intensely bright light coming from the left of my vision; it is like a pulse. If you can imagine the way a lighthouse beams light, well this one is pulsing the light like a heartbeat. Uriel says it is the heartbeat of our solar system, it is very bright.*

A: Tell me more.

J: *Then it pulses into concentric circles. He has shown me the image of a very large lollipop at a fair where in the middle you have a burst of colour. Then that colour gets dispersed the whole way through. Each planet gets issued a different colour, a colour wave of energy that responds to the beacon. The planets are on a particular colour frequency, humans are also on a bandwidth of colour and frequency, as are the planets.*

A: Can you see the different colours?

J: *At the moment all I am seeing is the intense pulse. Now the pulse of light has moved from the left to directly above me. They tell me the word photonic impulses. Like photons, something about photons being a light particle and that these light particles, these photons, are in everything.*

A: Where does that come from, where does that photon originate from?

J: *It's coming out from what looks like a black hole. In the middle is a black hole, then the brightness is coming around it. If you can imagine a very big black cloud on Earth, and if you had to punch a big hole with your fist right through the middle, in the middle would be the black hole. All around the edges of the black hole, the photons come down like rain. It is liquid light, as in beams of light and particles. There are thousands and thousands and millions of them, and they join together in streams of light, but they are energy, and that energy is within the actual photon.*

A: Can you tell me more about this? How does it affect the planets and the people?

J: *It energises them, the photons are the light particles, and the way they get assembled is what gives us our particular energy wave when they all link together in a particular pattern.*

A: Now, recently I have been working with frequencies of different types. Does this pertain to the same thing, the different frequencies?

J: *Yes, as we said with the planets on a particular frequency, as are humans with their photons.*

A: Wonderful. What happens when these frequencies are changed?

J: *Well, thought is a photon as well, so that is a form of energy. When the energy form changes, the photons are changing the pattern within that particular energy form, each energy form can manipulate or change its actual form.*

A: Is that why, when we have certain thoughts, it creates different realities?

J: *Correct, and that is also why you can change a cell structure within your bodies.*

A: So, for example, health and illness?

J: *Correct.*

A: OK, very good.

J: ***You can manipulate the energy in each individual cell structure by the way your thought process is attached to that particular body part.***

A: Now, when you started this, you began with the planets; you were going to show us the different planets. Can you tell me how the frequencies affect each one of these planets?

J: *Do you mean how the frequencies were when they are born? When they are created?*

A: For example, each one of the planets has its own frequency itself; planet Earth must resonate with its own frequency.

J: *Yes, it does. It is on a lower energy grid or a lower vibration than some of its brothers and sisters.*

A: Why is that?

J: *Because not all planets were born at the same time. Not all were created at the same time, some are older, some came out and were propelled at a greater velocity. Therefore, they were then created in a different solidity, in a different structure than Earth. As you have in a human family interaction between the different siblings and parents, there is an energy exchange, as are their energy exchanges within your solar system which creates a balance or an imbalance.*

A: I see, what is affecting our planet at this time?

J: *The actual thought processes of the beings that are inhabiting this planet affect it. As the beings and the energy forms on the other planets work in harmony or disharmony with the frequency that they are inhabiting, so each planet has their beings. Although humanity has seen a few of these energetic beings from distant relatives, their ability to interact and hold the frequency of their planets allow them more freedom than what is currently held on this Earth plane.*

So, on this particular Earth plane where you have a dense 3D body, and you are held by gravity, you are heavy beings. Often your thoughts are heavy, as well. However, you can lighten your load and your planet's load so that your planet can physically lift itself to a different space dimension and area.

A: Do we work with planet Earth to assist her?

J: *Well, there is a lot of talk about ascension at the moment. It is a symbiotic relationship; we would like to give you a simple example of parents and children.*

Parents come in and they host the children. The child lives off the human host for nine months before it appears on this Earth plane. Then the parents support that structure as the Earth supports all those structures called its inhabitants. But, like children, some don't always have a good relationship with their parents or appreciate what their parents are doing for them.

The children of Earth, meaning all inhabitants, don't appreciate what the Earth is doing for them. The Earth is the host for the human inhabitants and how are the inhabitants of the host treating the very host that feeds them? So, there is discord, there is no longer a feeling or no longer a symbiotic exchange of energy to its highest potential.

The Earth gets help from its brothers and sisters, as in a human family you would have what is termed, uncles and aunts. When you have a problem child the uncles and aunts and the grandparents get called in to assist the children when they are termed "out of control."

So, your Earth planet, which is also termed Gaia, has been asking for assistance for its unruly children from its brothers and sisters and grandparents in your solar system and also beyond. It's like an extended lineage for support because the Earth knows that they are in this together. The Earth is dependent on the inhabitants for its ascension and the inhabitants are dependent on the Earth for their ascension.

So, it's been a slow process. But those from the galaxy and the multiverses have been sending down those photons that we have been speaking about. Those rays, those colour forms, those energy forms are placed into the inhabitants of the Earth to change the vibrational structure within. The one that you are talking to today has just been working with James, Jesus's brother. He has been working within her structure, her energy form, for her to receive the information that we are transmitting for humanity today.

She is not alone in this job of ascension. There are thousands and thousands like her, that have opened themselves up for service for the rest of humanity, in order that the Earth and its inhabitants will be able to reach ascension.

A: So, why is it that all of these beings have incarnated at this time here?

J: *Well, that is why Uriel came through at the beginning. Uriel carries much light and will be working with this one in conjunction with James and her other guides. There are fractals of archangels distributed amongst many human forms at this stage who come from many other planetary systems to help. This one lies here today because she has her fractals on other systems within the galaxy.*

She could see that the problem child called Earth needed help. She and many others chose to come and assist; it was a call for help.

A: I understand that Dolores Cannon wrote books about these volunteers that came here. When you look at all of humanity, are there many volunteers at this time?

J: *There are many volunteers. In your organisations you have volunteers that go about their business every day without fanfare, gently working in the background. You do not see these volunteers. There are many more volunteers working in the background than those that are what you term a cheerleader, cheering the crowd on, being in the spotlight. It is what is called teamwork. Those football players, tennis players, those rugby players, those soccer players, all those teams don't become a team and play a game without the support structure of many. To be a team, someone had to train them, someone had to deliver them to the fields, somebody had to put the showers in place, have the kettle boiling, do the marketing, sew the team jerseys.*

So, many are very quiet in the background that are part of the team, and yet they never get attention or the glory, but they are just as important as the team players, as those that are seen on the surface. The volunteers on Earth, we say currently there are multitudes.

A: So, now that we talk about these volunteers, let's talk about the training ground for these volunteers. Who trains them? Where do they come from?

J: *They come from all over the galaxy because it is their family lineage that is here. So, when you have a team you will have not only one position that is being played; there are many positions on the team. Each team member is doing a different job. There are many different coaches or guides that are guiding the team members to do a particular job.*

A: Now, when they are being trained, these team members by these guides, is it in one particular place that they are being trained?

J: *No.*

A: How does that work?

J: *So, we would like to keep it simple and speak about the family again. You will have wise grandparents; those are on very ancient and old planets; they have gone through multiple times what the Earth is currently going through. They know what is needed, they know what resources need to be put into place. They know that it is their great great great grandchildren as such who will be the inhabitants. They know that diversity is what is needed for growth. So, they collaborated with their other grandparents, their brothers, sisters, daughters, uncles, and aunts through all the galaxies. They thought about what was needed for the diversity, for strength, for growth. For if you had one bloodline all breeding, then you would get a weakness because nothing new has been added into the pot.*

It would be like eating the same meal every day for the rest of your life. So, you need new ingredients. There was a call throughout the galaxies, throughout the multiverses. Those who had the qualities that were needed in particular positions on this big playing field called Earth were called to a meeting and it was decided within groups as to who would be best suited for a particular position.

A: Now, when you say it has been decided, did these volunteers have any say in them volunteering? Did they have free will?

J: *You know Alba, some children are good at some things and although they are good at it, they still don't want to get off the bed and go and rake the leaves off the garden lawn. Sometimes, a little persuasion was needed. Yet in other areas, they were so keen it was like they had to be held back until the time was right. It is no different than it is on Earth; everybody wishes for expansion and evolvement; some are just a little faster or slower than others.*

A: Now, you are speaking of diversity and diversity of the souls and their experiences. What happens when they get onto planet Earth? At this time, there are so many different issues going on between races, religions, cultures. Why do we have so many different cultures and backgrounds on Earth if it's going to cause problems?

J: *Well, there are many reasons for that. They have come and have incarnated into a form called human, but that is not their lineage. So, they come within a line, or a photonic structure carrying what you call DNA or a loop. This will differentiate one from another, but it will also remind them of whom they are and what they are carrying through from their home planets.*

A: Ah, OK.

J: *Although they have these loops, they are still human. The diversity is needed to teach humanity that they all come from a different lineage. Although they are part of a human race and a human adventure this time round, they have come with their different strengths to be united. They are here to help Earth get back into the family fold where it belongs, instead of fighting amongst themselves like children on a playground squabbling. They will eventually realise who they are and what they are working towards. When their photonic structure gets a little help from those that sent them here, they will wake up at different time periods, they will awaken when it is necessary to help with this evolution process.*

A: Is everyone meant to wake up?

J: *Some come as what we call or term "bystanders." They are like the support crew; they are not necessary in the whole scheme of things. Not all will awaken, but there will be a tipping point, and there will be enough of those that will wake that will allow the ascension process to take place. Those that are the bystanders have chosen to be bystanders. It is like somebody playing a part, an actress on stage. She will have what is called a stand-in. A stand-in will watch the process and will only step in if something happens to the actress. Yet although she or they are there, the audiences do not see them, so once again it is like a support crew.*

A: Are these bystanders on Earth? Do they have human bodies?

J: *Well, they have a human vehicle to move around, but they are not what we term fully charged.*

A: How would you recognise someone like that?

J: *They do not interact fully. They would be what you would term an outsider. There are many outsiders, and we are now showing her pictures of homeless people. Homeless are part of your Earth structure, and yet many Earthlings pass by them daily and see them not and yet they are part of humanity, are they not? So, if they do not even recognise the homeless as an equivalent, how would they then recognise a bystander?*

A: These bystanders, are they there to occupy space for us to make this world a reality for us?

J: *They drop in and drop out through the dimensions. They*

are there and then they are not there, and then there and not there; they are like a backdrop.

A: So, why is it that we live here on Earth? What is our purpose here, to come to planet Earth?

J: *For no other reason than to experience the greatness of who you are and to assist Gaia. She has had to learn how to interact by being the host. Gaia had to learn to balance many vibrations, many frequencies, on her surface. As humans evolve and different beings evolve, so do planets. As we have to lift our vibrations, so does Gaia, so we came to assist the Earth as the Earth assists us.*

A: OK, but that sounds like on a much higher level than for those humans living life-to-life. What do we live for here, I mean, I know we came here to help Gaia, but what is life all about for us as a human?

J: *Life is about a particular photonic structure. It is about knowing one's structure and understanding who one truly is. Most humans do not know who they are. They have a 3D body. Many of them have a family, some choose not to. They trace what is termed a family tree, but that family tree is not their true family tree, for they have many forests (family tree branches) but not all of them are on Earth. The life on Earth, specifically on Gaia, is to learn who they are.*

For when they are in their other forms on the other galaxies in the multiverse, they are very aware of who they are. They come to live on Earth to learn who they are.

A: What is the easiest way for humans to learn who they are?

J: *We have spoken to this one before about the point of stillness. Humans are called a human being and yet so many think they are human doings because so few of them just be.*

Until you find the point of stillness there will be lots of "doingness" and no "beingness."

When one is quiet and reaches a point of stillness without all the distractions, then everything, all the answers are found within. You know, Alba, this one was with you in Peru in March of this year, and during what you term a gathering through a guided meditation she had to walk through three imaginary doors. One of them was so bright that it was the brightness that she saw today of the evolution and creation of planets.

She was told that she was the light that held the galaxies together and linked the galaxies. Afterwards, she found out what we meant when we gave her the term "galaxy." We said each human has an entire galaxy within them.

So, the photonic patterns and vibrations are that of a galaxy within each human as they are "being." So, what pattern do they wish to create? Do they wish it to be light or do they make it condensed? Each human has a choice.

A: Thank you. We also spend a lot of our time on Earth talking. Can you tell me a little about our voice and how that affects the photons?

J: *We told this one about a "portal of light," which is your mouth, your mouthpiece, your sound comes out of your mouth. Sound, frequency, light, are all photonic. Each human has a voice piece and a sound. For those that are what you term mute still make their unique sounds. We spoke about choices and stillness and being.*

When what comes out of a human's mouth is of detriment to others it will be of detriment to themselves. When this happens, Alba, it is because the human has not been still. They have not held the conversation within. They have not put in what you term any thought. So, as a result it is thoughtless as it comes out of their portal, and it is no longer a light portal, because it is now condensed.

Why would humans not take the time to be still and hold the conversation within?

When they do not do this, it comes out as a heavy form. It then damages not only themselves but others. For many humans it takes many human years for them to learn this. This one that is speaking for us today; part of her mission is to teach people exactly that — how to use their portals with their photons so that their life is lighter and easier.

For as she does this work through you, there will be many then through these words which are being dictated today, that will for the first time realise how their voice boxes work. Their words are so important, and so the ascension is helped. The whole process through this process that you are using today is helped.

A: So, as we continue with this, let's follow that voice. Where is that voice coming from, is it coming from the human or is it coming from elsewhere when they speak?

J: *It is coming through a form called telepathy. Through a pathway from source through this one through the portal. It then gets interpreted by many through their perception. That is why when one speaks it is not always received in the same manner; sometimes, the messages get misunderstood.*

A: Why is that? Why is there confusion? Is there some sort of breakdown in the technology of the words?

J: *No, there is no breakdown. The receivers are either having a dense structure or a lighter structure. Here is an example. If their structure is dense and tightly woven, it would be similar to having a castle and a moat and very high walls so people would shoot their bows and arrows and their guns at the castle wall and it wouldn't penetrate because there would be a very deep heavy wall, it could not get through. And yet, if the walls were not up, those arrows would hit the mark. So it is with humans and their hearing. They choose to hear it a certain way by putting up their walls until they choose otherwise.*

A: What I come across a lot are those that have been victimised by others, by their words, by their actions; a lot of emotional and verbal abuse. Can you speak to me about that, how people use their words to hurt others?

J: *You know, victimisation is such a slow process. That is why the work that you and this one does through your hypnotherapy sessions allows the client a peek into their subconscious, it allows them to see the part that they have been playing which no longer serves them, and it is so helpful to them.*

The reason that there are so many victims is that, once again, they do not stop and take time to go within. It is more convenient to blame another than to look within. For when one looks within, then the true work begins. They are like a child; they are in adult bodies but they are still acting like children. It is time to grow up and see who or what they are.

This one, Alba, was taught a lesson specifically about being a victim, and her husband played his part so well. For many years she felt so sorry for herself, until one day we orchestrated it that it was time for her to wake up to do the work that we wanted her to do. The lesson of being a victim was one of the largest lessons that we gave her so clearly that she will be able to change so many, and it was done in a very humorous way.

She has learnt that this part of growing up, this part of ascension, has many side players. No one does it alone. Her son, husband, herself, and a friend played a part in this for everyone. When she returned home from that particular weekend and from the lesson, she still did not realise that she had been given a lesson until she played a podcast called "Do you lie to yourself?"

As soon as she heard the podcast she got up and apologised to her husband. He wanted to know why, and she started laughing. She saw how much time she had robbed herself of by playing the victim. She said to him, "I have just discovered that my voice box resides in my throat, not in yours. I can speak up for myself, but I didn't think enough of myself because I did not know who I was", so I blamed you.

That is why the victim role needs to be opened up and shown for what it is. Victimhood is nothing else other than lack of self, lack of value. Once humans understand their value, there will be very little victimhood being played out again.

A: Do we pick these roles even before we are being born?

J: *Some do, some don't. Some choose the roles for evolution.*

A: How do you know if you have evolved past this victimhood? Is there a way that you can tell that you have mastered that?

J: *Yes, it is part of a photonic exchange that when the person is ready to no longer play the game, for it is a game, they then get a new photonic structure, a few extra lengths, which then enables them to receive clearer communication and therefore that role is no longer necessary.*

A: Where does this connection come from?

J: *The photonic downloads?*

A: Yes, is it coming from source?

J: *It depends on each being. Some will get it dropped through the lineage from their other planets, from their beings that are in their group that are helping them. Some get it designated at a particular time within the part that they are playing in the human game, as to the harm they are doing to themselves and those around them. It happens specifically to wake others up, to annoy another to such an extent that they have enough. So, it is not all bad. Others will get it from their source structure, depending on their evolution from their angels, from their archangels, from their guides, or directly from source.*

A: Can we expand a little about those that help us, the guides, the angels? Did we choose them, or did they choose us? How does it work, and what is a guide?

J: *As I am seeing this, I am seeing huge brightness from above, which is what I saw when we first started. That incredible light that comes from source, and as it comes out, it comes out like a meteorite, lots of sparks. Some of the sparks are bigger and hold more energy, and some of the sparks are smaller, in shorter little bursts. It's almost as if the bigger sparks look after the smaller sparks. So, the bigger sparks have more energy, hold more potential and surround the little ones.*

They come out in little groups or clusters, and within that group they embody the role of guidance. Does that explain it?

A: Yes, but do the guides get trained to be guides? How do they know how to guide? Is there a structure within the guides themselves?

J: *When they come out of the frequency of their original creation they are created with, I am seeing the most incredible light form, it is like the shape of a leaf, it is glittering and it is gold and its silver and it's not within all the sparks, so it's like having a good gene.*

They are showing me that you have families on Earth; some are very good athletes, other families will never be athletes — they just do not have the build — so you have to have that specific light particle within you, embedded in you right from the beginning, for you to be a guide.

A: Are there different levels of guides?

J: *Yes, because there are different levels of energy.*

A: OK, so how is it that the guides become our guides, is there an agreement?

J: *Some of them see potential and then choose to work with certain potential that is aligned within them. It is like a frequency or a grid pattern. They can see that by guiding or nurturing a particular energy form, those will actually fit into their grid pattern which in turn helps them to evolve as well.*

So not only are they guiding that particular energy form, but that energy form is symbiotic, again working with that guide to evolve and expand that guide as well.

A: Do we only have one guide that stays with us or are there other ones?

J: *Some energy beings might not wish to work with a particular guide; they may feel they are not quite ready for that particular guide. They may work with a lesser guide until they feel they are ready to then move up to what you would term a higher level. So, it is a choice as such, it is not dictation.*

A: Does it work both ways then? You can pick a guide and vice versa, or the guide can pick you?

J: *Well, the guides certainly pick you as such. The guides will have communion with each other as to which lot of beings are going to be passed onto the next step. It would be similar to a whole lot of children in kindergarten starting school for the very first time. First-year teachers have different natures so the children from kindergarten will be best suited to a particular nature, so you would not push certain children under a certain teacher, you would choose the teacher suited to them for their best progress.*

A: Does it have anything to do with what type of form or incarnation we take on? The attraction for these guides?

J: *Yes.*

A: Can you tell me about that?

J: *Well, if Alba is an Alba and she has her guide for her human incarnation, her energy structure is different to that of being on Andromeda; her evolution in another form will require a different guide.*

A: Now, that leads me to expand even more; are we living different incarnations at the same time?

J: *Yes.*

A: Can you explain to me how it is that one's soul, let us say the soul of Jill, how is she living in different places with different forms?

J: *We have told you that she is part of the Galactic Federation of Light. She is also on the outer ring of Saturn, on the forum of 49, she is a human, and parts of her visit Arcturus, Andromeda and Sirius. There is also a part of her that is a scholastic traveller at the same time as a human; a scholastic traveller is a scholar through the galaxies. That part of her dips in and out and goes back to the fullness of who she is. The other parts all have different guides, but then they report to the highest guide working with all those guides, for the evolution of her soul, or super-soul.*

A: Who is her master guide?

J: *Urka*

A: Can you tell me a little more about Urka?

J: *All I'm seeing or being told are geometric patterns, and there is light everywhere. Previously we had a black hole and the light on the outside. This time, the light is on the inside and the black is all around it. Urka is working with the highest of the high.*

A: Which we term "source," or is there something in between?

J: *Urka has a direct line to source and then it goes through all the sub-guides, and then to all the participants, like a telephone exchange.*

A: So, where does our higher self fall in between all of that? Is that our soul?

J: *Think of an obelisk and a capstone that is on top of the obelisk. Your energy vehicle would be the obelisk and your higher self would be the capstone. On the top of the capstone is the tiny little sharp structure that would be your beacon, your receiving point, which then connects with your guides and each particular incarnation as the photonic frequencies increase. As this occurs the guides that you may have will take a lesser place, and you will get a new guide stepping in to be able to work with the higher frequencies.*

A: Is that what has happened to Jill?

J: *Yes.*

A: OK, now another question about the soul. Do we have a different higher self for each of the incarnations in different places, or is it one higher self for all of them?

J: *Some energy forms don't have what is termed a higher self, as they are in direct communication through that frequency with Urka. A human form works differently, as some are denser.*

A: I see it like a substation, something smaller and denser that needs something in between to communicate.

J: *Yes.*

A: Very good. So, talking about the soul, I know there is a lot of talk about soul family, can you explain what a soul family is?

J: *When we spoke earlier about the guides coming through with the meteor, with the huge shards of light, as that burst comes through the initial creation and it disperses from the one to many on the same frequency range, that then is a soul family.*

A: Are the guides part of the soul family, too?

J: *Correct.*

A: OK.

J: *That is why they are aligned to your frequency.*

A: OK, now that we understand that we fall into that family, what do we do with that family? Do we incarnate together? Do we work on things together? Tell me what it is that the soul family does.

J: *The soul family are always there as a support structure, also to rein you in when you are going off direction.*

A: Do they stand in for the guides also? In a way, do they guide us?

J: *Within a soul family some choose to go into different timelines together, some choose not to. They may decide to become a different etheric being at that particular time, and so those that are enjoying human incarnations together will go back to base to discuss what it is they have learnt, and where they wish to go to on their next adventure, and push each other, show each other how they could have done better, help each other. Then they welcome home those part of their family that have gone onto other multiverses, but they always regroup in a particular place.*

A: Is this what we would term the council?

J: I'm not sure I understand your question.

A: Well, there are many times that we see a soul after their incarnation goes to a council where they discuss their life. Is this part of their soul group?

J: *No, that is a substation.*

A: Can you tell me about that?

J: *There are collective beings with a particular skill of what you term assessment. You will have one wise being from your soul family sitting on that council where your particular group go, and an assessment takes place, and it is a support. For one is assessing oneself rather than being assessed. Once you have gone through that, you go through your portal to your family group.*

A: Can you tell me about this portal that you travel through? Is it within your soul, or is it outside of it?

J: *No, it is outside of it because you are still coming through as that old energy form. It is just a particle of the soul.*

A: We find in many of our regression sessions souls that do not go towards that portal, that they are afraid. Can you tell me a little about that? What happens to those souls that don't leave this dimension?

J: *Those souls are never unsupported, for they are part of the grid system. That connection is always there, although they cannot see it. The support is held in place for them until they are ready to see it. Just like we spoke earlier about the walls that people put up so that they did not hear correctly, these particular souls, or rather beings, have not gone back to their soul groups and soul families because they cannot temporarily see the line that is connecting them.*

But although it takes time, the work that you and this one are doing, and many others are now doing are reconnecting or connecting the lines of communication with these souls that have been trapped on Earth. You are showing them their way home, for those that are part of their soul group or soul family need their soul groups to be together for them all to evolve as a group. That's why they are never alone. It is in the interest of that group to get all the group members back on the bus. They cannot go on to the next destination until all the group members are back on the bus.

A: Are all the group members being dispersed at the same time, or is it like different fractals of the personalities coming together? Do they all go and do incarnations, or do some stay behind?

J: *Often, a group will decide to go to a particular spot. It would be like a family saying, "Hey, guys, where are we going to go on vacation? Let us go to Hawaii," but perhaps the baby is teething, so the mother says, "You three go, you go to Hawaii, but I'm not going to Hawaii just yet. I will come with the baby in a week," so the mother and the baby stay behind until they are ready.*

A: When we pass from this human body through the way station, is there a time when we just take a little siesta or a little vacation from incarnations?

J: *There are some in the group that are what you term workaholics, like you have in human form; they don't take a holiday, they just push and push and push. These are the ones that take new life forms, new energy forms, and sometimes they go back before they are ready. They think they can cope, and then a few problems appear. Sometimes, they have a short life span and think, well, that did not work for me; I should have taken that siesta after all, that vacation. So many have favourite spots where they have been before, and that's where they go; they go globetrotting.*

A: I see, recently, I have been reading some books about some places which are between this realm and the spirit realm, where the spirits help those who are leaving Earth. Is this a place that truly exists, like a spirit hospital, where those go to rest before they even go back to the council?

J: *I'm glad you asked that question. That was the only one question that this one had on her piece of paper today that she did not give to you because she felt sorry for you. She felt you were writing so much down. She did ask in the question that when a body, a human body, passes away on this Earth plane through terrible disease and then goes back to All That Is, did that body need healing? Yes, there is a way-station.*

Please to know that there are many way-stations throughout the dimensions, for there are many different beings. So, the Earth has a way-station. These particular places called way-stations have light that comes in colour, where the beings have a transition, which to them would look as if they were in a human hospital, but without walls, maybe just rows of beds. They would be receiving showers of coloured light and particles of what they need to reconstruct and make themselves what they term, healthy and whole.

They are there for some time. That is why often when these departed energy forms communicate with their loved ones left behind, they usually show themselves in their thirties, for that is usually when they were at the peak of their energy.

Once their human vehicles have been left behind (old energy) they are given what we term a, what is the word I am looking for, it is like a service, it is like giving thanks to the human body for being the vehicle, it is a last goodbye.

Not all humans need this, but those that were particularly diseased from what you may term cancer where their bodies have withered away and they are still holding on to that humanness, once they know that their bodies are strong, it is easier for them then to connect with the council for the overview, before they then join their soul group or their soul family.

A: Now, those are the ones who thought that their bodies have died in terrible ways, but what about their mind? What do you say about those people who have no faith, no hope, I don't believe in anything? Does that affect their transition out of their human body?

J: *Well, that is when they are met by their human loved ones who were deceased before them. They gently take them to a place of beauty and stillness, be it in a forest setting or a small cottage, something that they are familiar with, maybe a pet dog or a cat or a horse, whatever it was that they were familiar with in their humanness, and as they are there they are gently coaxed until they have a remembrance, none are lost.*

A: OK, so, now once you are in the soul once again do you have a yearning for more? Is there a yearning there for those that may not be workaholics, but is there a yearning?

J: *Each guide that one is given knows or reads the energy pattern of that energetic being. They know in which direction to point you. It would be like a child not really wanting to do the exams, but then being told that unless they do the exams, they are never going to become that particular artist or musician that they want to be. It is going to open the door to that special exciting part, so that is where the guide has incredible mastery. They can literally shine a light and give you a little peep, like a trailer before a film gets released. They just pique your interest. Those who wish to take a vacation or a siesta, they do, but how long can one be on vacation for?*

If you look at what has just happened to humanity with this Covid virus, where you have been locked down and locked up. In the beginning everyone enjoyed the seclusion. But if it went on for six months, a year, two years, well the novelty of that seclusion would wear off. So is it such with evolution; one cannot remain stagnant for long.

A: You talked before about us having multiple incarnations. Is the energy the same in each one?

J: *The energy is more in some and less in others, because some beings are what we term streamlined. Humans take up a lot of energy because they come in 3D. They come very condensed, very heavy, so it takes more energy to run the system. Whereas other beings from other dimensions often use telepathic means. As a result, they don't use the energy. They don't need what is called human food to fuel the body, therefore, the fractal that they get incarnated into requires less from the mainframe.*

A: So, how is human life, do we have more?

J: *We have more.*

A: There is a term called "an old soul" here on Earth, can you tell me what an old soul means?

J: *An old soul, all souls are given opportunities, some reach their potential quicker than others. Those that wished to go on siesta did not take the same class at the same time period as the old soul, so the old soul is not better than one that has not taken that class, for there is no competition.*

That soul that is not as old as the old soul will get to the old soul's time period, if you want to call it that. The old soul may be an old soul in human evolution; it may have decided to have many incarnations in the human field, however, it may be a very young soul in another galaxy, having very little experience in that arena, and then the young soul, that you think is a young soul in the Earth plane, may not prefer to do their lessons on this particular plane, but prefer somewhere else in the multiverse, so, therefore, how does one compare?

One seems to think on Earth that if one is called an old soul that one is somehow special, better than another, and this is not so. We would like this to be known.

A: Does it also have something to do with how many incarnations you have had on Earth?

J: *Yes, an old soul is because they have had many incarnations on this Earth plane, but you could be an old soul in another galaxy, having many incarnations in that particular form.*

A: Those that come here to this Earth now who seem to be young souls for Earth, it seems that they are constantly wanting to go home, that they are yearning to go back home, that they don't like this Earth. Can you discuss that, please?

J: *They do not like it, because they know of another way. They are not here for the lower base levels of humanity, the competition, the detriment, the putting down, the division. For they know another way, for they are very connected to the other way.*

Their remembrance of the other way lies within them greater often than those other humans. Although they were part of the group that volunteered to come and help with the ascension process, it is difficult for them. Some of them feel the pull to home very strongly, so they terminate the human experience, and they go back home.

Alba, there is no judgement on those souls because it is nothing but an experience, and what they wished to experience.

A: Do they have to come back to finish off that experience, or are they done with it?

J: *It is a human belief that if you don't learn a particular lesson that lesson will reappear, but it is between the council, the assessment, the guide, and that energy being. Sometimes, the being, because it is living within a different energy system, forgets what it is to be in a human form. It forgets the denseness, and they feel that they will be able to cope on the Earth plane. Yet the reality of living on the Earth plane as opposed to that other lightness of being is what you term "chalk and cheese."*

Although some were guided not to come back to the Earth plane so quickly, in their haste for evolution they disregarded the guidance because of free will, and came back and found out the guides were correct, and so they go back.

Some stay, although it is painful for them and hard for their family members because they fight against it so much. These people would be well suited to guidance from one such as you Alba, to show them that they have chosen this particular lifetime, so you can help them find the joyful bits and their life mission, for all have a life mission. When those that wish to go home get reminded of their life mission, then many of them are alleviated of their dark thoughts, because now they see the light on their path.

A: Does their soul choose their life mission, or is it picked for them?

J: *Both, a soul group can decide as a group to go on a mission, a particular mission, or individuals can volunteer, or, because of their qualities, they can get chosen.*

A: Is there a headquarters for your soul, a place where your soul resides with all the information?

J: *Yes. It is part of All That Is, source keeps all souls. If you can imagine source having cells, cell structures. Well, a soul would be like a cell in the All That Is, so you are part of All That Is. You are part of source, and therefore you are always connected to source. You then leave source, and although you leave the nucleus of your cell, the outer wall of source's cell is your mainframe. You then disperse into your lifetimes, and so source can feel every experience that you undertake, and so source expands, source feels, source connects, as do you.*

A: So, would that be like our mainframe where everything resides?

J: *That would be your mainframe, protected by source.*

A: How can we access that mainframe?

J: *Through the point of stillness.*

A: Is that why they tell us to meditate more?

J: *Correct, that is when you Earthlings are at home, when you meditate; then you know who you are. For although you might be a human form on a bed, on a yoga mat, on a couch, in a chair, on the ground, leaning up against a tree, your physical body is there but your soul connection is travelling through the lifetimes.*

Similar to a fractal of Jill, of her soul talking to you in another country called America, and her in New Zealand, you are talking over what is termed airwaves, so it is no different to you being able to connect with your home base.

A: Wonderful. Now, recently I have heard of something termed the God Code which they say is within each one of our cells and our DNA. Is this true? Are we connected to what we call our God, or our creator, within ourselves?

J: *You know, Alba, it is strange that you bring this up. Well, it is not strange, but it is very aligned that you speak about this with this one. This one was told that her God Code has now been turned on. Her God Code has been activated, and because her God Code has been activated, she now can activate the God Code in others.*

The work that you, Alba, and this one is now doing through your airwaves, through this book, you will be activating the God Code within many, which in turn will then help them to activate others, help ascension within themselves, as in Gaia, and as in your entire solar system, within a giant matrix, so each and every player plays a part in the evolution of one another.

A: I intended to be the instrument of God; I say that often. As my videos go out around the world it seems to be awakening something in people. Is this what is happening when they are seeing others? Are they connecting with that part of themselves?

J: *Alba, this one has now told you about the cell structure of God, source, the one, call it whatever you like. As she has her headquarters there, as you have your headquarters there, she has used the analogy now of the rampart where the arrows could not get through the wall, and there are many that lie dormant, too scared to break through. What you are is an activated light encoder. Your energy frequency sound is what is used as the key to activation. It is your ankh. Because of your vibration and this one's vibration, you are now opening the hearts of many who listen to what it is that you are saying. For, Alba, without your skills and ability, those that you have been hypnotising would not be reverberating to the masses.*

We would like to applaud you for your mission, for you have embraced your mission, and as a result you will get satisfaction as you open up the satisfaction in others, and as this one's mission is to teach people who or what they are, that is exactly your mission as well.

A: Wonderful. Thank you. You know you spoke about the voice and that is something that Jill was questioning. They say that the fingerprint is unique to a human; what about the voice? Is that also unique?

J: *Your voice is who you are, because it differentiates you from another. Your voice is your energy, your voice is your photonic structure. There is no one with your voice. So, we would like to say, what are you doing with your voice? Are you using your voice as a weapon, or are you using your voice as a gentle stream?*

Your voice is one of the strongest parts of your human system. For many bodies get diseased or crushed or malformed, and yet you still have a voice. Many are in wheelchairs, many have disfigurements, but they are what you call "motivational speakers" and how do they reach the masses, Alba? With their voices.

We do not wish the voices of humanity to lie low.

This time in the time of human ascension is the time for your light portal to be open, and for your words to be used. We wish for humanity to go into their point of stillness. Once they have connected with themselves through their line of communication to source, and when they have listened to that voice, what is it that they wish to say?

How do they wish to be governed? How do they wish for this Earth to be? To then remember that they are part of what is called, a human race. Now they understand why they have differences, because of the different lineages which make them stronger to come together as a community, and a collective called humanity. These are the lessons that they need to learn. To work together as very strong links on a chain, so all may evolve forward. Thank you, Alba.

A: Thank you very much. May I ask who we have been speaking with today?

J: *Urka*

A: Very good. Thank you so much. Is there any message that you have for Jill or me or anyone in particular outside this discourse?

J: *We put you and this one together just a few human years ago, and look what has happened from your connection. She, through her sister, brought 49 humans together to learn hypnosis. You both went and met your soul family in Peru. What happened to you and this one in Peru were new strands of photons, an energy pattern being laid down, a new grid-work. By working together, you have formed a very strong pattern, for as one holds an individual pattern, one can hold patterns with another.*

As Alba you have a pattern with one called Antonio, you have another pattern with one termed Blair, you have another pattern with this one. All producing different work, working together for humanity.

We know that this one has been treading water, knowing that she had something to accomplish, but she could not see what it was or know what it was.

When we showed her on Wednesday the nature of her mission, for the first time in many years this one felt what you term "complete." She has now contained herself in self, she is now self-contained.

She can see her path, her cell in God. She now sees her God structure; she now sees the God in her. She wishes that this body of work will show humanity that God lies in all.

A: Wonderful. Thank you so much for this. Are we complete for now?

J: *We are complete.*

CHAPTER TWO

STRUCTURE & MULTIPLE LIVES

In this hypnosis session Jill speaks about DNA and our fractals in other galaxies, that we travel through dimensions and timelines holding different forms. When we die, our energy is reunited with the area from whence it came.

A: As you get closer, I want you to notice what is the first thing that you see on the other side, is someone there for you?

J: *Not that I can see.*

A: All right, so I want you to begin to drift into this beautiful place and I want you to create a beautiful landscape in front of you. In this landscape I would like you to create different archways made out of stone. I would like you to see below your feet. As you begin to walk, what does it look like under your feet, what do you notice?

J: *I don't feel that I am actually on Earth, I see many archways, and they are coming towards me at an incredible speed. It's like I am travelling through the archways, but they are in another time and space. It's similar to going on a very fast train and you are traveling through a tunnel at hyper speed, then there is a burst of light, then another tunnel, and another burst of light, that's what it feels like.*

A: I would like you to continue going through those archways, and I want you to pick the direction that you want to go today to find the answers to your questions. Which way have you chosen?

J: *The archways have all converged like in an old-fashioned Tupperware jello mould. If you can imagine the archways are all around the jello mould, each individual one takes you right through into the centre point, almost like a vortex or a torus field, and if you go through the middle like the doughnut part, well that is where it is pulling me.*

A: So, as it is pulling you into this, I want you to tell me why is it that you are going to this spot today. What's there?

J: *I hear the word centre point.*

A: Very good, focus on this centre point. What comes to mind?

J: *It's huge pulses of light.*

A: Are these lights any particular colour?

J: *Well, if you look in the very centre it's almost like the colour of a pupil of the eye, like the all-seeing eye.*

A: Can you get closer?

J: *It's concentric circles coming out of that. It's similar to dark golden rings that are transmitting, they are transmission waves coming from the centre point that are going up and out in every single direction.*

A: Find yourself in the middle of one of those waves so that you can receive the transmission.

J: *It looks like it's on top of a mountain, a mountain top. It hits the top and then it waves out.*

A: I want you to use all of your senses now and tell me how that feels.

J: *It pulses through me, lots and lots of short bright pulses, wave after wave.*

A: Allow those pulses and waves to begin to make changes to this body that is travelling, so that you can begin to feel as if you were a receiver of the waves. Allow this to begin now, use this body, this mouthpiece, as the instrument to relay the information that we are looking for today.

J: *OK, so they said that the information from the centre point radiates out and it picks out the mountains for humanity. The mountains are like the capstones, like transmitters, just like a beacon for each individual area, and it is a conductor, so it is helpful for the humans in that area, different mountains hold different energies.*

A: Where is the energy coming from? Can you tell me that?

J: *From the centre point.*

A: This centre point, is this part of our galaxy?

J: *No, it's deeper.*

A: If we were to go deeper into the centre point can we get more information?

J: *You will only get the information that you are aligned with.*

A: So, what is the information that Jill is aligned with today?

J: *She is on what's termed a "superhighway", she has many lines that are open for communication. If you look at a colander and run water through a colander, all those streams of water that come out of it, the multiple lines, she has multiple lines, multiple streams of connectivity.*

A: Jill had a few questions that she wanted to ask today; can we begin asking those questions now?

J: *Yes.*

A: Most important one to start with is about intuition. I know that when she is in hypnosis, she needs to use a part of her that connects. When people speak about intuition or their gut, what does that mean?

J: *You are connecting with your neurotransmitters; it's coming to you as a warning system. As you on your Earth plane have a road sign ahead with a red flashing light, it is a special impulse that is sent to you to recognise, just like a beacon flashing, telling you there is danger ahead.*

A: Can you tell me who sends that information?

J: *The connectivity to All That Is. It sees everything, knows everything. It knows what's ahead before you know what's ahead, as a human. It sees what is about to happen, so it sends in the light brigade. Literally, the light brigade comes in to assist. Therefore, the light is enhanced in that particular area and in that particular moment. Because there is more light, it is like you are literally lightening up and seeing in that specific second or moment. That is why they now tell me that we have a connection because we are all connected.*

If you have a child in danger, they can see that the child is in danger.

Although the child may be living many miles away from the human, the connection is there, the mother immediately knows something is not right because literally her antenna is up, and it has been switched on. This human talking to you now had problems with her Bluetooth this morning because she wasn't turning it on and connecting it correctly.

A: So, this intuition you are saying is coming from the All That Is. But where do the guides and the higher selves fit into all of that? Do they also help?

J: *They are part of the conductors, but the currency and the vibration that travels through you will sometimes come directly from source, to them, to you, as we explained in an earlier session about being the switchboard.*

A: When we speak of free will and intuition, are there times when people do not listen to their intuition?

J: *Yes. We have explained to this one that there is a human terminology that is used, saying that when you don't listen it comes back to bite you in the bottom. Humans say, "Oh, we felt that, but we ignored it. Oh, is that what it was?"*

So, it is teaching humanity to receive the impulses that are the vibrational frequencies that they feel at any given moment. It is like a child that wants to touch an iron, and you say, "No, do not touch it, it is hot," but they do not listen and then they touch it and say, "Oh, the iron's hot."

So it is when we send you the impulses for the warning. The intuition or the gut can pick up the impulses or the vibration and they ignore it, and then something happens and then when they get that same feeling again, then it's, "Oh, that's right, that's what it means, that's my intuition," so it's a learning process.

A: What about when you use your intuition with people? There are many that say, “I can read their energy.” Are we using the same thing, the intuition? Are we reading them, or are our guides telling us “back off. That’s not the person to be around”? How does that work?

J: *You are reading the energy, you are tuning in. If there is an energy different to yours and it does not flow, then you will feel it in your body, you will know in seconds “this is not for me, this is not my vibration, this is not my wavelength” and then, once again, many will go against what they feel, and they will have what you term a bad experience, it is in order to teach them once again.*

A: When we are with another person and we just don’t feel safe with them, stay away from them?

J: *Listen and stay away, because that is your antenna and that is your beacon saying, “danger ahead.”*

A: Very good, thank you, are we born with this?

J: *Correct, it’s part of your wiring system, it is your programming.*

A: Is there a way that this wiring system or programming can be damaged?

J: *Yes, there are those that interfere with the system.*

A: Who are those that interfere?

J: *These are from other areas, other galaxies, that don't wish the program to run smoothly, for they have a different agenda.*

A: Is there a way that we as humans can fix that intuition if we know that it is happening?

J: *We spoke to this one. She had an experience with a being wishing to interfere with the agenda and the programming. They were trying to circumvent this channel and trying to close it down. However, she was aware of it because she had risen and changed her photonic structure and vibrations to experience what we termed the other day "light and dark," which means nothing other than "rising above like a feather or a bubble," or dark, meaning "heavier, dropping down." So, as the heavier vibrations drop down, it does not allow you to use the higher; it starts to close off the higher.*

For example, if you had human fingers on a piano and somebody dropped the lid down, you would not be able to play the piano as well because your fingers would be constricted until someone lifted the piano lid, then you could start playing beautifully again, so is it with vibrations.

She had had some fresh codes laid during a meditation session and this interfered with those dark beings' agenda, they did not want the fresh codes there. So that evening during her sleep, she was aware that something was interfering with her system and it woke her up. Because she was aware of them, the replanting of their old codes into her was unsuccessful.

She was then taught about what we term a "Merkabah" or a "Light Body" and she was taught to think of two golden triangles, one above and one below, the top one spinning clockwise and the bottom one spinning anti-clockwise. She was sitting in what we term the "Magic Square" connecting the two, and with these speeds, they would cut those cords of communication from those that were trying to lay the implant.

We taught her that this is called cloaking, and it is what your guides use when they come to communicate with you. Most of you do not see guides because of the cloaking. We wished for this one's ethereal and etheric and her multi-bodies to be cloaked from those who wished to interfere, and as we did that, we cut their cords of communication, but not ours.

A: Is this a technique that can be used by anybody?

J: *Yes.*

A: Great, thank you. Now, talking about multi-selves, she had a question. Many are now understanding that they are multi-dimensional beings and there are no such things as past lives, that they are all happening at the same time. Is this possibly how it works, that we have different lives at the same time?

J: *Different energetic experiences.*

A: Different energetic experiences. OK, so are they all happening at the same time, all of these energetic experiences?

J: *Well, when you speak about time, could you define what you see as time?*

A: Well, let's say right now Jill and I are speaking together. Are there others of us, in different dimensions, different places, doing different things?

J: *Yes.*

A: OK, so, at any point, do all of these come together?

J: *But those others that you talk about of "us" are not Albas or Jills.*

A: Can you explain that, please?

J: *When we spoke to you last time, we spoke to you about you being a cell, and your cell being called a soul in the organism of All That Is. That the cell divides into multiple fractals and those fractals are energy. All are part of your oversoul. It is the soul that is over all the souls that then incarnates into many multiple beings simultaneously, and because their energy structure is in a different vibrational pattern to that which you take as human, it will be running on a different frequency and in a different, what you call dimension or level.*

A: Can there be multiples of you living at the same time, let's say Earth years?

J: *You mean multiples of the fractals of the cell?*

A: Yes.

J: *Because when you say of you, no. There are not lots and lots of Albas living at the same time, but there are many fractals from the cell or the soul of the one called Alba, Alba is just one of the slivers. So, yes, there are multiple Earth lives or Earth energy frequencies, they are nothing but frequency outputs.*

A: OK, so when we do a past life regression, can you tell me what it is that we are speaking with, or viewing? Is it the different aspects of us?

J: *It is actually a current life regression, and is it really regression because where are you regressing to? Rather, are you not travelling through the dimensions and the timelines.*

A: So, it's semantics; it's the way we speak about it, it doesn't make any sense?

J: *Correct.*

A: I have always envisioned it like a DVD with everything happening at one time, just pointing the laser to a different place. Does that make sense?

J: *Your analogy is very good. If you think about a CD, you have one human called Celine Dion and she will put out what is termed a CD and there are many songs, are there not, on the same CD?*

A: Yes.

J: *None of those songs are the same, and yet are they not on the same CD?*

A: Yes.

J: *Do they not jump from timeline to timeline on the actual CD?*

A: Yes.

J: *One minute to three minutes to four minutes as you term time in human form, and yet they are on the same CD.*

A: Wonderful.

J: *Each one holds its own energy and its own vibration.*

A: Do all of these different songs on these CDs, do they ever become one again?

J: *Well, they are one, they are the same CD.*

A: Does it go anywhere else? Does it become anything else after that? Is that CD part of a different type of CD, a bigger one?

J: *Well, it is actually part of a CD collection.*

(Jill and Alba both started to laugh at the comment.)

A: Can you tell me something about that?

J: *So, you have your fractals, your CD collections, and they are all gathered playing their beautiful music. We could also term this a harmonic convergence. Do they all play at the same time? They certainly do, and their sounds that they emit are all different, all orchestrated beautifully by the conductor, and the conductor is the All That Is.*

A: Now, when we do hypnosis sessions, we usually go to a point in that person's past, which we now call the CD, in which perhaps there has been a scratch there that is affecting all of the songs on the CD. When we go back and fix that scratch and make a change to it, does it affect all of them, even the collection?

J: *I think there is a word that humanity uses called marred. But there is no such thing as imperfection; everything is done as it should. We have had this conversation before, that if you fix one do you fix and affect them all? Yes, all are affected in a different way because it runs through the collection, through the vibration, and yet it is not a problem, for it is as it should be, for what you term a problem is not seen as a problem in the overall scheme of things.*

A: How is a challenge looked at by the soul?

J: *Growth.*

A: Growth.

J: *Yes, growth and expansion.*

A: Very good. Can you speak a little to me about death? Many humans avoid this subject, however, each person that will be listening to these words or reading them will die, and many believe that they will meet Jesus or God or Allah after their human body dies. Is this true?

J: *Well, firstly, the body as such dies or disintegrates, whether it gets eaten by worms or it gets burnt in the fire, depending on how they wish to dispose of the vehicle that they used for their souls, or fractals experience and expansion. So, once that is what you termed "laid to rest," a thanksgiving or a funeral is held and many speak about the human personality that inhabited that human vehicle, that human host, but very few ever give thanks to the human vehicle that played the part of the host.*

So, once the host has been disposed of, the energy of the fractal is then reunited with the area from whence it came. The belief system is part of the programming of that energy's experience, be it Hindu, Jewish, Zoroaster, Christian, whatever it may be. As it goes to its way-station it will then meet the energy that helps them with the transition as in their belief system.

A: So, if they believe in Jesus, for example, will Jesus meet them? Are they creating Jesus in their own belief?

J: *They are creating Jesus in their belief system, for if you speak to many humans who say they go back to God, and ask them, well, what does God actually look like? often they don't really have an answer for that or their perception of Jesus. There were no photographs taken in the time of Jesus, so it is something that they have conjured up in their gallery, that lives in their mind space, along with many other images that are held, for if you had to ask a Christian what Allah looks like, how would they answer that? So, as you can see, it is something that has been manipulated by the programming of belief.*

A: What about those who do not believe in an afterlife? They just believe they are a body and when they die nothing else happens. What would you like to share about that?

J: *Well, they are in for a WILD RIDE.*

A: Can you tell me about that?

J: *Well, these are the ones, many of them, who are termed a trapped entity, who do not immediately return via their way-stations, for they don't even know that a way-station exists. They will be roaming around the Earth plane in what they think is a human body, not understanding what it is and why it is that they cannot be seen — it is what you term a ghost — until they come across someone such as you, Alba, or the many that practice what you practice, releasing them back to the light, or they have help from what you term above, which is not really above because it is on the same CD, and they come in to assist when that ghostlike apparition or Earth-trapped being in that form starts querying and asking for assistance.*

A: Very good. Thank you. Now, going along those lines, there are many that feel that the light is a false light, that this light is something that is manipulated by other beings to keep us in a trap. Can you tell me what this light is? I always see it in my mind's eye as a light within yourself and when I tell people to go to the light, I'm always envisioning a light within yourself. Can you tell me about this light?

J: *Well, that light is what we termed earlier, is your God Code, for it is encoded within you. So, when you ask them to look for the spark within, that is their GOD SPARK, their light. We have spoken before of the word ankh, which is encoded with their light, which is your DNA, your loop. And that is where your many lives are, in your DNA, in your light spark, that is where this is held, and that is why we say, go within, go within.*

A: For those that think that reincarnation is like a punishment, where we are trapped here on this Earth going round and round, what would you like to say about that?

J: *Well, they did the choosing. What do they choose?*

A: OK, very good.

J: *If they choose not, then it is not so.*

A: OK, so it is our free will to come back here?

J: *Correct.*

A: You have talked to Jill before, saying that humans have the power to will a dead cell to life, are you able to share this process and how we can do that?

J: *Yes, it is about the photonic structure that we discussed last session. Everything is patterns, which is vibration. We once showed her a steel plate with sand on the top, and then the steel plate was plugged into an electrical output. The steel plate when switched on moves at a certain speed, and the sand particles jump up and down and form a pattern. So, if you want a different outcome you have to change the pattern, so you turn up the velocity and more sand jumps up and down and the pattern changes, so this is the same with your thoughts.*

So, when we said that you can will a dead cell to life, you are all cells, are you not, with multiple fractals? That cell can never be dead, but it can be what you term, the walking dead.

You are slumbering. When we say will a dead cell to life, we are saying it is time to wake up, wake up the cells, wake up the fractals, wake up the humans to their potential.

They have these what they term diseases, through the mind structure of belief. Why is it that on your Earth plane when a doctor tells a patient they have three months left to live, that so many live for only three months? Because it is what someone else has told them, and then it becomes their belief.

A: If this is true, how come there are those that defy that, that live longer?

J: *Because these are the ones that believe in self, have more strength within to change that vibrational pattern. We do not wish to make a judgement on this day, for there are many that have what you term "a use-by date", and for them, it is but their time. We would like to use this as an example of the ability of the human mind.*

We do not wish to denigrate any humans that have been given three months by their doctor, and then lived only three months. We are not saying that those in particular were weak, or weaker than a counterpart, because it could be their time, but it is time for many to realise the power of not putting the disease into their cell structure from the beginning.

A: Now, you have spoken before about freedom and power. How can we ensure that we don't lose either of them? Can you perhaps clarify that, where you can see that happening in our world, losing our freedom and power?

J: *You know, this one spoke to her husband last night, quite agitated about freedom, and his response was, "But you are free. You are in a free country, you can walk anywhere you like without anybody restricting you, you can say anything you like without anyone restricting you."*

This was partially incorrect for although this one lives in what one terms a democratic country, there are people's rights being slowly shut down in this country and in many other countries, and whenever you hear the word conspiracy or conspiracy theory then you know that those people are being shut down.

When this happens that is not freedom, and one needs to ask WHY do people need to shut another down? What is it that they fear to lose by shutting another down? For if all are honest and true, should there not be an honest and open discourse for all to see?

So, therefore, when your freedom is eroded then you begin to lose your power base, and this is a time for power bases to be amplified, for we see the erosion setting in throughout your Earth domain.

A: How do we get that power back?

J: *By uniting with each other, by questioning everything, by investigating, and as we began this conversation, with your intuition and your gut and your antenna we are sending many flash warnings.*

Antennae should be up throughout your Earth plane.

You can see there are many new groups standing up and asking questions. They speak over many platforms, they speak about sovereignty and sovereign rights, about the rollover, roll up, roll out of what you term 5G. There are scientists for it, there are scientists against it. So, where is your panel, your open discourse of all these specialists on one panel, live, for the whole world to see?

You now have what is termed vaccinations with your Covid that is out. Where is the open discussion? For many humans are now fearful. They have been placed in a state of fear from the very governments that are there to protect them. Why are these people so nervous, what is it that is making them nervous?

We always say "KNOWLEDGE WILL SET YOU FREE.".

So, is it not time once again for all the specialists, instead of competing against each other for the one to be the first for the vaccine, why do they not all have an open platform with all the information that they have, as to where this came from, why it is here, and is there really anything to be fearful of?

There are many that are implying that the vaccinations that are being spoken about are filled with many detrimental items such as toxins that are toxic for the human vehicle that you have got, as your host to experience your expansion. Yet these very vehicles, your human body, is being damaged by foods, by vaccines, by radioactivity.

So, one has to ask oneself, what is the end agenda? Whose agenda is it? One must ask the leaders, why are we not allowed to have an open debate without chastising or talking down or belittling those that wish to have the open debate? For if there is nothing to hide, then there needs to be an open debate on all sides together.

It is time to peel away the layers, and let us see what lies beneath.

A: Wonderful. Now, you have given us, or kind of walked around this virus. Is there a spiritual reason for this virus, something that perhaps all of us as one has created?

J: *That is very well said, Alba, and very intuitive of you. Your antenna must be on high alert.*

(Alba laughs.)

J: *When humanity sent their vibrations to a level of asking for change, bringing about change, wanting a different way, wanting what they term a new world, and harking back to the way it used to be when people had time for each other, well, as they say, be careful what you wish for it; may arrive in a form that you had no idea it would.*

We told this one just before she saw you for the very first time that the great leveller will arrive, and it has arrived. The great leveller who treats all the same. For it is a time for rebalancing. It is also a time for enquiry, for has it not brought up many discussions across the board?

A: Yes, many are happy that they have time for themselves but there are many that are upset because they are losing their businesses and their homes. They are not able to live the life that they had before. What do you say to those who are so distraught about not being able to function, or to feed their family?

J: *What it is to be human, as opposed to another fractal on another dimension, another galaxy, another multiverse, is what you term "emotional output." Happy, sad, angry, fearful, jealous, revengeful, greedy, egotistical, arrogant, lazy, exuberant, all these have emotions. What these humans are forgetting once again is who or what they are, so they are living an emotion, which in the larger scheme of things is a very small moment in time, but they came specifically to the Earth plane to experience emotion.*

Now the emotion of losing a job creates a certain vibration within that steel plate once again. When one gives birth to a brand-new human form, the emotion is totally different to losing one's job or one's livelihood. One did not come onto this Earth plane to experience just joy the entire time, or pain the entire time, those emotions come in waves.

Yes, many will lose their livelihoods and then they will reinvent themselves, and then they will go back to the All That Is, they will go back to the way-station, and then there will be a discussion as to how they fared, how they coped with what was presented to them.

Many at this time will try and blame someone else for what they deem as a loss, but, when they came onto this Earth plane they came with their arms and their legs and their mouth and eyes, and their little human form, and most of them will leave that way.

They do not arrive with their business degree, with their house, with their cars, their cell phones, with their clothes and diamonds. When they leave, they do not leave with those either. They come in as an energy form, and they leave as an energy form. What happens between the living and the dying is all on loan. So, be grateful for the moments as they arrive, for at any given moment the next may be withdrawn.

A: Thank you. What do you say about those that are coming with different ways of being? Autism, for example, and allergies.

What is happening to the human form? Is this a change? Is this on purpose? Or is there something that is happening on Earth that is changing the body?

J: *Your Earth is changing as everything changes. There are many new chemicals that are being introduced, not only onto your ground, onto your earth, over your plants, but now also into your air.*

All this affects your central nervous system. The cell structure for your skin is a large, breathing organ, and everything seeps into it. So, everything that you breathe, everything that you eat, everything that you walk on and over, affects you.

There are many thousands of new particles that you as a human being now have to adjust to that you did not have to adjust to, thirty, forty, or fifty years ago.

The new beings (babies) that are being grown and incubated within the mother, well, whatever is in her system gets filtered through into that new energetic form, and within some are disturbances. That is why one of the factors that is known on the human plane is alcohol, and why new mothers or pregnant mothers do not drink alcohol, as it affects the foetus. So, there are certain things once again that need to be discussed.

What or who are you giving your power away to?

There are many adjustments that need to be taken, there are many governments that need to be addressed, for they need to be given a dressing down.

A: Talking about that steel plate, I am thinking about the vaccines that are given to children and adults in order to ward off disease. If you are saying that our thoughts change the composition of our bodies why do we need vaccines?

J: *You don't, but you have been led to believe that you do. For those that are manufacturing the vaccines do not know who or what they are. They are here to experience as you are, and their experience is not your experience. So, once again, we would like to ask you, how many vaccines is a child in the year 2020 being given by the time they reach 16 years of age, as opposed to those ten years ago, twenty years ago, thirty years ago? Why is there a need for these new vaccines? Who is driving it? What are the driving factors behind any given situation?*

A: Now, some of these vaccines, can they affect some people detrimentally and others not at all?

J: *There are some that are termed a stronger constitution. It depends on their genetic code, of their lineage that they get.*

A: So, some will get affected and some will not?

J: *And that is why.*

A: OK, good. Can you tell me a little about food? Some humans eat meat, others are vegetarian. Can you explain to us what is the effect on the human system? Is one better than the other?

J: *This one heard a terminology when she was in her early twenties. It said, "you are what you eat, dead meat," and yet she still imbibed. The amount of energy that it takes to be a carnivore is of larger consumption than that of a vegetarian, so once again, it is a choice. What does one choose? The lighter load or the heavier load? One will always expand eventually. Do you want it to be quicker, or longer? Do you want to rise higher, faster? As they say, choose your poison.*

A: Recently, someone wrote to me saying they needed to eat meat because they wanted to be strong and grow stronger. Is that a belief system?

J: *It is a belief system, and they will retain it until they decide otherwise.*

A: So, it is not necessary to eat dead meat?

J: *No, otherwise how do you have strong vegetarians on your Earth plane? They would all be walking around with walking sticks, would they not?*

(Alba laughs heartily.)

A: Can you tell me a little about what the Earth is going through right now? We have been told that we are going through a process of ascension and that there are other planets and people from other galaxies watching us. Is this true? Are we being watched?

J: *Yes, you are being watched through a viewing platform.*

A: Can you tell me about that? That sounds interesting.

J: *On Earth, you have something called Skype, do you not?*

A: Yes.

J: *If you have a child living in another country or another city and you wish to see their face, you cannot unless you use FaceTime or a video or Skype, then you see that child's face. So, you have those from the other galaxies that have a vested interest for the Earth plane, for this is their lineage, for as we told this one, many are star-seeded and they wish to see their children grow, how they are developing, it is a family concern.*

A: Many who are seeded are always crying out, saying they want to go home. Does this have anything to do with the connection of those watching? Are they influencing them, making them homesick?

J: *There are some that you term babies. In real life, they don't really like leaving the nest. They eventually go on their journey and create their own families, but there is nothing like going home, having Mum doing your washing, putting on your favourite meal, and this one has been removed from her homeland in Africa, for she married what is termed a foreigner, she is now living away from her home base on the Earth plane, although this is not her true home base.*

Yet, on a winter day or over a Christmas period she will get what you term homesick, or a longing for that particular spot of comfort. It is just temporary; it shows that there is great love there, or they would not feel this had they not been nurtured and comforted.

A: So, what would you say to those star seeds that are so homesick?

J: *Is it not good that they actually have a home base? They are here on an adventure. Just imagine the discussions they can have when they go back. For the generations before them were what you term pioneers, that went out to the newly-formed planets and seeded them initially, and so it is a cycle.*

A: Good. Now, we talked about those that are watching us that seem to be benevolent because they have seeded us here, but what about those that are not benevolent? Jill has a question; is there life on other planets, for example, Mars? Are we being abducted by those from other planets?

J: *There is life on Mars as there is life on many other planets.*

Once again, there should be an open discussion about what you term alien or alien abductions, for in many of your government institutions you have what is termed classified files. Once again, why do these need to be classified? What is it that they are hiding? If everything is open, honest, and true, why can this not be shared? When they are not shared, this then opens up rumours and conspiracy.

Why should there be a conspiracy in the first place? Who has been conspiring? Who conspired to actually make this classified?

So, yes, there are many Earthlings who know what is going on in other planets and have communications, have technologies. Sometimes the technologies get traded and are being traded at the expense of some sectors in humanity, but, Alba, with the vibrational pattern called ascension, much is being lifted. Soon much will be exposed and then those that started the conspiration will have to explain why that is.

A: Is there any way that those who could be abducted could be protected in the future?

J: *This is where free will becomes a bit complicated, because with free will and choosing experiences, at what point did that energy say I'm going to Earth and I'm going to open myself to experience anything, and then at that stage that this then opens that being to experience things that they weren't ready to experience?*

So, maybe what needs to be taught is how to retract the contract within.

Say, "I am ready for experiences as long as they are not to my full detriment," or being able to change that at some stage.

A: Going down that same path, can you explain to me what the numbers 666 mean? We know that it adds up to the number nine and they call it the mark of the beast. What is that, 666?

J: *I'm seeing intense pulses and it looks like lightning everywhere. It is an intense vibrational pattern, and it seems like it's some kind of control system, it looks like a war. I am being told a war in the heavens, and that has something to do with 666. It is interlinked with incredible warfare.*

A: Can you hone in and see who are the ones that are warring with each other in the heavens?

J: *I am getting "tears from heaven." It is almost like something has gone rogue, something has gone skew or amiss, not part of the plan.*

A: Is this what they are saying is the new world order?

J: *It is like a rogue element, a blip in the program. It was not supposed to be there.*

A: Has someone actually created this blip?

J: *Aaaahhh, now it looks like the light is directly above me and it opened up. In our last session, we saw the shards coming through when they were created, like soul families, and it's like it is a bad seed. You know when you talk about a bad seed in a family, yes, it's almost like it's a bad seed.*

A: So, is it a bad seed in humanity?

J: *It is like it is there from the beginning.*

A: Now, being that everything is like being on a CD, was this placed on the CD or was it placed afterwards?

J: *No, this is from the beginning.*

A: Did creator have anything to do with this seed?

J: *It seems so.*

A: For what purpose would a creator create something like that?

J: *Duality.*

A: Contrast.

J: *Yeah.*

A: Does that help humanity to grow in any way, or evolve?

J: *It says something about the dark and the light. How do you see the light? You place the light against the dark, so darkness in itself has a job to do.*

A: Is there any type of co operation with those that assist us? For example, the divine beings of the light, the archangels, do they have anything to do with that darkness or seed?

J: *I just see now that it's like intergalactic warfare as such and all those archangels are standing right in the front with all their shields up, shielding. Then there are all the Earthlings behind them in the distance. It is like they are protecting them from the dark. Once again, they say it is a battle for the souls of humanity. It is like a big chess game; each player makes his move and humanity are the pawns. Then there are those that are working with the dark forces, for they have temporary riches, temporary power, and this is what fills them up. They keep on needing more because it is not coming from the inside, it is coming from the outside; it is not coming from them. It does not come from within, it is something that is bestowed onto them, for doing something against another, so it's actually like an addiction. You know, if you have a candy, then you need another candy and another candy, and before you know it you are 300lbs. It all comes from the outside.*

A: Is this just from Earth, or is it way beyond Earth?

J: *Earth is just a substation, as I said. This is just a small, small player, rats and mice. We are just the rats and mice, really.*

A: Is any of this warfare affecting our physical Earth? For example, they talk a lot about climate change, is any of this affecting the actual Earth?

J: ***The Earth has always gone through climate change.***

This is called "cyclical." It is how it changes.

A: Is there a purpose for that change?

J: *It is similar to taking a shower. Clean everything off and have a fresh start. The next day you feel so much better. It's not stagnant, it is changing. It is also evolving and expanding and lifting.*

A: So, it has nothing to do with the people on it. You are saying it is the way the Earth shifts and moves.

J: *The Earth is able to clean itself, and this is a part of how it cleans itself.*

A: OK. Is there anything that we as humans need to be concerned about at this time?

J: *Well, it is going to happen. Whatever is going to happen is going to happen. If you spray a dog with a hose, or put it in the sea and when it comes out how do you say do not shake? Is it going to stop shaking?*

A: We say it many times; don't shake. They shake, regardless.

J: *Or wind, don't blow.*

A: So, these things that the Earth is going through, for example, the melting of the ice and the shifting around, is this going to happen in our lifetime?

J: *We are not at liberty to say.*

A: If you are not at liberty to say, how can we prepare ourselves physically, mentally, emotionally, for the changes that will naturally occur with the Earth's shaking off?

J: *Well, this is the whole purpose of this conversation, Alba, between you and this one. We are having this discourse in order to open people's minds to different things. Different ideas, different thought patterns. To maybe think:*

What is a star seed?

What is a multiverse?

What is a way-station?

What is a guide?

What is intuition?

What is death?

What is vibration?

What is frequency?

Who am I?

What am I?

Oh, I am a fractal of light and I travel between the galaxies and the multiverses. Do I really have anything to fear? Whether this Earth explodes, whether it gets covered in water, whether there is peace, whether there is war, I am observing it as I am watching a film. But I am in the film, I am one of the actors, and this is the part I am playing. Do I like my part? Am I good at my part? I am part of the cast; the directors cast me in this role, and it's a role that I have chosen.

I arrive with my soul family or part of my soul family, or as a solo journey. Soon, it will be over and then I will be on another adventure. I am currently having many adventures; this is but one.

Humanity always likes to see what is going to happen instead of living now, making the best of this moment, which will then create a better moment for the next moment. They rob themselves of moments by always looking to the future, for if they do that, they are not living fully right now.

We do not wish to place fear in any human form, for we need the vibrations to be high for a peaceful and smooth transition period. That is why, Alba, we commend you and this one for this work, for putting it out.

So that as the troubled times draw nearer, and things become clearer for many, they will have a knowing of who they are. Then, they can stand in that power and have peace, rather than fear.

A: Good. Thank you so much. Is there anything else you would like to say, or would you like to be complete for today's session?

J: *Alba, I think we are more than complete.*

A: Thank you so much. Until the next time, thank you again. Will you tell us today who has been assisting us? Can we call you by a certain name?

J: *Urka.*

A: Urka. Thank you very much, Urka, until the next time.

J: *Thank you.*

A: An honour.

CHAPTER THREE (Session 403)

THE AWAKENING

In this hypnosis session Alba guides Jill back to a dream in which she saw both of them working on a mission together. The session continues with information and questions asked of a high-level guide with whom they have been working on a special project.

A: What is the first thing that you remember from that dream as you're looking at all of those screens?

J: *Invasion.*

A: Invasion, tell me more about this invasion.

J: *An invasion is being planned, so we at headquarters are working out a strategy to protect our fellow star-seeded beings.*

A: I'd like for you to notice who else is there with you doing the planning.

J: *Well, you are to the left of me, Dean is to the right. Sabrina's there, Bettina is there. Laura's coming in, Laura's coming in through the door, its sliding open, she's coming in. That's all I see with them.* (These people are currently living on earth and are Jill and Alba's soul family. Many met for the first time when they visited Peru in 2020.)

A: What are we wearing in this place?

J: *You've got leggings and a long, beige tunic.*

A: Notice if there are any insignias or anything on our clothing?

J: *You've got a triangle on your arm. It is a triangle, but instead of it completing, it goes up a little bit, sort of like a triangle and then up on the inside.*

A: What does that mean?

J: *They say triad, we are part of a multiple force, it is intergalactic, three huge galaxies. We're part of two other galaxies working together.*

A: What are these other galaxies that we work with? Do they have names?

J: *One sort of sounds like Endotropia, Miloaxia that is what it sounds like.*

A: Milo-Axia, very good. And what do we have to do with the planet Earth?

J: *Well, currently we have a shield in place, protecting them, but there are those that are now finding weaknesses in the shield, trying to get through and interfere. We are sending out teams, like investigative teams into those areas. Sabrina is in charge of that. Sabrina called the sub-council and is getting the troops ready. The teams are going on the outskirts all around the shield, looking for the areas that need fixing.*

A: What kind of shield is this all around the Earth?

J: *Well, it is a very thick protective shield that we have put in place. It is energetic. We have shown this one before that it is like a honeycomb structure, because that shape, that design, is the one which has got the strongest bracing.*

So, the other ones that want to come and interfere with the Earthlings that this one spoke to you about the other day, about how when she was in a meditation session getting new codes implanted, that she was disrupted that night with a being wanting to lay their codes in her. But we managed to get her to be aware that she was being interfered with, these are the breaches we are talking about.

A: Okay.

J: *They are interrupting the programming of the human's communication. So, when that communication is disrupted, then they are controlling the humans on Earth, and then this is interfering with free will.*

A: Now, this honeycomb shield that is around the Earth, are you able to leave Earth through this shield? Is it a one-way or a two-way shield?

J: *It is high above Earth, there are areas like a trap door that we can come through and some of these areas have been breached.*

A: Can you tell me more about these that are interfering with us right now? That seems to be the talk these days, of how things are getting out of control. Is this part of it?

J: *As there is ego on Earth, there are some beings that are very advanced in what you term a technological manner, however, they are having to work through their ego, and it is an ancient rite in them, as in an R I T E, like a ritual, where they have a lust for power and control.*

It is something that they have not managed to overcome at their point of evolution. So, they have a need for warring, and as a result, many galaxies have banded together in order to fight, or try and stop the penetration of this particular warring nation of beings.

A: At this time, we are seeing a lot of demonstration and a lot of warring within my country. Do these that are invading, do they have anything to do with that?

J: *Yes and no. We spoke last time about power and freedom and about 666 and a rogue seed. Now, there are those on Earth that fill themselves up from the outside and do not connect with source, the superhighway that you and this one has. They rather fill themselves up with what you call "material goods", but this is not lasting. So, they fill themselves up then with power and control, and these are the ones, the factions that work behind the scenes, that feed — literally feed — the demonstrators. Those that demonstrate have no idea that they are being manipulated by puppet masters.*

A: Now, these puppet masters, is this anything to do with what is termed the New World Order that people talk about?

J: *This term New World Order has been used for many years, as in when you had your old war, which was termed your Second World War, they were then talking about what it would be, to be in "a new world."*

As you presently were harking for a better world to live in, to spend more time with family, Covid appeared, and those from the Second World War were also talking about how it would be to have a new world.

Those puppet masters have now created a new world, but they wish it to fall under their order. And so, it is a new world, and it is being ordered in a particular way.

A: Can we also talk about ascension, the spiritual ascension? Is this also part of the new world, or is that something new?

J: *Yes, what has happened is your humanity is now reaching a tipping point, where the puppet master's strings are now being tangled because they are not pure of heart. They follow the external, they do not have the spiritual bond that you who are on the superhighway have. As a result, there is very little trust, as you say, amongst thieves.*

There's a saying in humanity; "give somebody enough rope and they will hang themselves." These puppeteers have got extreme amounts of rope, and we say watch this space.

A: So, as this is happening, this hanging of themselves, can you tell me what it is that we as souls, Jill, myself, Sabrina, Dean, all of those that are on another level, what it is that we are doing that assists humanity?

J: *We want to take you back to the CD. So, Jill, Alba, Laura, Bettina, Dean, who are now on that ship operating and co-ordinating help, are currently dispersed on your Earth plane as Earthlings as you know them. Their energetic vibrations in the other fractals that they are, are also linked to the beings on that ship.*

Because they have that energy, it is like a transmission and a transfer, so they are able to co-ordinate in different ways on this Earth plane, as they are simultaneously organising what we term a search and rescue operation from that ship.

A: Very good. Would you consider that ship a timeline? Or is that just a different fractal of our soul?

J: *You have a different energetic being within that ship, but that ship skips timelines at will.*

A: Can you explain to me what a timeline is, and how it is that it skips or jumps timelines?

J: *A timeline is a warp, at warped speed. We told this one that all you need is a sliver of a fly's wing in order to jump into another timeline.*

We would like to take this opportunity, Alba, if you do not mind, in helping humanity with their time, and timelines.

A: Thank you.

J: *So, this one was travelling through what is termed Cardrona Valley or the Crown Range, and it was a quiet evening, no one around. She was doing 50km and she could see the 70km zone about 100m ahead. She put her foot down ready to go home for the evening when suddenly she saw a traffic cop. He saw her, and at that moment she knew she was doing harm to no one as there was no one around, and she asked us for assistance.*

She said: "Is this really how I need to end my day? It's been such a perfect day; it is such a beautiful evening." She very facetiously said, "Can't you just make them disappear?" Then she just carried on driving, expecting to see the traffic cop in her rear-view mirror. But we granted the request and put a warp through time. When she looked up, there were lots of cars coming towards her and lots of cars behind her, although she had been the sole traveller on that mountain road. She could not understand where all that traffic arrived from.

She thought, "Where did it come from?" When she got home, she had a conversation with us, and asked us what had happened, for she knew that something untoward had happened.

She had what you term "an experience." We explained to her that a timeline is something that you control, because the future, the past, and the present are all happening at the same time. This is something that you haven't understood yet; humanity struggles with this. But if humanity is having what you call "a tough day", you can actually request the time to speed up. Conversely, if you need more time because you have so many jobs, you can ask for the expansion of time, and so it is granted. This is what happens when one knows who or what one is, but most humans travel through their days aimlessly, totally unaware of the supreme beings that they are.

A: Thank you. Although this was not part of Jill's questions, right now it seems that I am shifting timelines myself. The person I was just several weeks ago is almost on a different path. Is that what's happening with me right now? Am I shifting?

J: *As you say this, Alba, this one lying on this bed has suddenly got a vibration from her pubic bone travelling all the way to her breast bone, in intense waves. We mentioned photonic downloads in our first two sessions, and this is what has happened to you. Your physical vibration has been lifted, the weight of your 3D body, your matter, had been of a heavier load, and your star-seeded lineage knew the work ahead of you and ahead of this one. As a result, both of you had experiences at Peru at the same time, for we wanted both of you to open up into the fullness of who you truly are* (Jill at this point in the session is overcome with emotion). *Jill is now seeing the power of who you both are.*

We spoke about vibrational patterns of the alignment between you and Blair, and you and Antonio, and the work you do with those ones. And now the pattern, the link on the chain with this one, for one such as Sabrina spoke about the light army that you are building, we have waited a long time for this one to wake up.

We mentioned ten years ago the discourse with this one. Now that she has found her life purpose, through this purpose and the alignment with you, the lightness of who you are now, needed to be incorporated at the same time as we "popped her cork."

We needed her mouthpiece to speak through your platform Alba, with your team and our team working together. It is a very large body of light that carries this work forward. Alba, the discourse is just the tip of the iceberg with the work that you and this one is going to be able to achieve. As you work together on this platform, this platform will just grow and grow, for this is very important work, and the timing of this work is imperative.

This one has been treading water for a very long time, and we did not want this timeline to be steered in a different direction. But we told her many years ago that she has extreme discipline within her very nature and yet she could not see it, as she did not have the excitement of seeing the vision and the knowledge of what it was that she needed to do. Although deep in her very being she knew that there was something else that needed to be done, she didn't know what it was.

So, Alba, that is a very long answer to your question but, yes, you are not the same being that you were, as when you entered Peru, as when you exited Peru, for your light particles, your photonic structure is now on a higher vibration.

When we spoke to this one about the sand on the steel plate being plugged into the electrical output, we literally have turned up your volume. You need to be heard, Alba, loud and clear. That's why we turned up your volume.

A: Okay, very good. So, the sensations in the body that I'm feeling and the motivation to get moving is all part of that?

J: *Adjustments needed to be made. Where you are, you are living in what is termed "old energy." Did you not feel the need to do what's termed a painting job in your apartment?*

A: Yes.

J: *The reason that you needed to do that was literally to wash away the old energy, for that energy was no longer part of your vibrational pattern. A move is imminent.*

A: Is that why I'm being pushed so much?

J: *Yes.*

A: Thank you for that. Can we talk more about Peru and about Jill's channelling? Because she feels that whatever we went through in Peru, if we were to go to Egypt for example, she would experience even more, can we talk about that?

J: *This one is correct when she feels a pulling towards Egypt. She had no inkling about Peru prior to the suggestion to go there. She had heard about a place called Machu Picchu, but although she lived a lifetime in Peru with you and her soul family that she met on the Peru trip, her real home base in human terms is in Egypt. She has had many incarnations of incredible power and wealth in Egypt.*

When we speak of wealth, although she has wealth in material form, we would like to speak about her wealth of knowledge (Jill is once again overcome with emotion upon hearing this) *for did we not say that she was the gatekeeper of the portal of Egypt? For when this one returns to her home base in Egypt with the others, a true activation unlike anything that you have ever witnessed will appear, and her power will be shown for all to see. There will be no doubt left for any who have ever doubted this one before.*

A: Wonderful, thank you. Now, in Peru, she was channelling. Who was she channelling?

J: *She sees them now.*

A: Who are they?

J: *They are the light force, the angelic realm, this is her team.*

A: Do they have their own language?

J: *She is part of the angelic realm. We spoke through her in an ancient Peruvian language as she spoke to the gods that looked over the harvest in that arena, but she is a powerful being of light.*

A: Very good. Is that why she saw wall-to-wall angels in that tunnel of light that summer's day long ago?

J: *It was her brothers and sisters showing her how when they join in their vibration of alignment, that humanity is escorted home through their tunnel of light. The angelic realm creates the tunnel of light for humans to pass through, when it is their time to exit the Earth plane.*

A: Wonderful. So, if she is part of the angelic realm, can she do something like that with those that she works with here on Earth?

J: *She can.*

A: How can that be activated now?

J: *We activated her when we spoke about the God Code in the last session.* (At this point in the session Jill's voice changes as she begins channelling a different energy.)

The reason why we talk the way we are now transmitting, is we spoke about the God Code being activated through many and, Alba, you will be showing this session to humanity, and as they hear these vibrations so they will feel the emotion shift, as it has shifted in this one. This day, they will be unlocked.

(In order for readers to be unlocked, they will need to watch the video session on YouTube to receive the vibrations. It is session 403, The Awakening.)

A: Wonderful. Thank you so much. As one unlocks the God Code within themselves, what can we expect? What changes?

J: *More disruptions, disruptions for humanity. We wish for the GREAT AWAKENING, so the transmissions need the activation to occur. For those who are activated know who or what they are, so they do not react with violence or anger, but rather with a deeper understanding, that this is a process of ascension, and it is a birthing pain. However, you and Jill are what are termed "the midwives" and you are helping them with a smoother transition.*

A: Thank you for that. Now, Jill, talking about her again, channelling, the first was the angelic realm, the angelic channelling. What was the second time that she channelled? Who was she channelling?

J: *There are those who doubt this one, this one still lives to please, for she did not know her power, but she was speaking directly to us. There will be no doubt in her mind after this transmission.*

A: Wonderful, so, was she speaking as herself? Was she channelling this higher version of herself?

J: *She was speaking through her brother, Archangel Michael — Miguel.*

A: Wonderful, thank you so much for that. What about in the future? She was wondering if she's going to be channelling more, and will it be in English so people can understand her?

J: *We will be transmitting through this one in many languages.*

She will be travelling the world, Alba, you will be at her side on many occasions, for this one has the ability to speak in any Earth language that we dictate, and she will reach those who need to be reached.

Time is of the essence; we wish this work for you and this one to accelerate. These transmissions need to go global. Yes, there will be a book but these broadcasts need to be broadcast as soon as possible. The time is quickening. We spoke about this one hearing the trumpets, those trumpets are mentioned in the Bible, those trumpets are being heralded.

(Jill is overcome with emotion when she hears this.)

She is one of our heralds; she will trumpet. She spoke with Jesus, and one of His disciples, Peter, and He asked them, will they continue His work that He started many years ago? She has now embraced this mission.

Alba, we would like you to climb on board this mission. You are an imperative link to this very important chain. Will you accept this mission that we request of you this day?

A: I accept this mission now.

J: *Thank you, Alba, so be it. James, Jesus's brother, is working through this one. He is opening her physiology in order that the sessions ahead be thorough and be clear as crystal, for we wish these ones that work with you, and specifically, Alba, this one, who is our messenger from source, to be very clear, that there will be no further misunderstandings, that she is part of the chosen few.*

(Jill was gasping for breath during this part of the transmission.)

A: Thank you.

J: *There are many, but there are few. We told her that she was part of the ancient ones. She was part of the original seedings of Earth. We wish you to hear her words.*

A: Thank you. Would you please give her a deep breath so she can relax and allow those words to come out much smoother? Give her a deep breath, allow her to breathe. That's it. Very good. And with that calm now, could you tell her more about this mission? Should I continue with her questions?

J: *Yes.*

A: Thank you. You spoke about Jesus. I'd like to ask a little bit more about Jesus and about what he learned and how he learned what he did. She wanted to know about the Essenes, and if Jesus was part of that.

J: *Yes, Jesus was part of the Essenes as was this one, and part of your group (soul family) that went to Peru. The reason the Essenes were working in seclusion, were that many wished to shut them down from what you term the "Judaic" realm, for they were working with an old energy. Yeshua, Jesus, was working through a direct line to source, as this one, as we said earlier, is on a superhighway with many, many, many connections. Jesus had that highway, those connections, and so he was able to understand what you term, "the bigger picture."*

He was not one for power or control. He could see the light-workers, the army of light-workers that he needed to resurrect, for they were slumbering as many in humanity are slumbering now. When they spoke about bringing the dead back to life, Alba, you and this one will be bringing the dead back to life. For they are alive, but they are dead, they are slumbering and they need to wake up. So, he formed a group called the Essenes, with his brothers and his sister and his very special Mary, and James, his brother, was his close confidante.

A: His brother James! Did he have brothers and sisters? Was James an actual brother?

J: *Yes, although many in this realm speak about "Hello, brother," "Hello, sister," especially in what you term "the new age" where they like to call each other brother and sister, but this was a genetic bloodline of brothers and sisters. This one that you are speaking with today was Joseph's sister's son. So, Jesus and this one were cousins.*

A: Okay, anybody else that we know of that were part of that

Essene group?

J: *Yes, Alba, you were this one's granny, you have a very strong bloodline connection with Yeshua.*

A: So, was I his great aunt?

J: *Correct, correct.*

A: Now, I've seen how people have talked about how I was always there with Jesus, and I've seen myself during those talks.

J: *You were the wise one. Yeshua used to hang onto your skirts as a young boy, as did this one. You were very gentle and kind, as you were through many lifetimes, and are now, after Peru, being more aligned for the first time in this lifetime.*

We are bringing you all together again. Jesus is sitting as this one said, on many councils, and He sits with her His cousin, on the Inter-Galactic Federation of Light, and that is why he sent her as a "Jill", to be his peace ambassador on Earth, in this lifetime.

He sent his great aunt to be the collaborator, to carry out the work they set up as Essenes. And this one (Jill), grew to be a great teacher alongside Dean (Dean is part of Jill & Albas soul family and went with them to Peru) during that time period, called the Essenes.

Currently, on your Earth plane, there were books that were hidden in a cave called the Dead Sea Scrolls. One of your group, I'm being given the name Donna, (Donna is also part of their soul family and also went with them to Peru) *she has a connection with Jesus. She was a scribe; it was her information that lies within the Dead Sea Scrolls. That is why this one has had a fascination with wishing to unlock the Dead Sea Scrolls in this lifetime.*

A: Now during Donna's hypnosis session with me, she saw us there, and she saw the marriage. Did Jesus get married?

J: *This knowledge will be upsetting to many and yet it is true. Although many at this time, at this Earth time wish to think of Jesus as a god, as God's son, and yet he was flesh, he was bones, he was a man. My cousin had a great and deep love for Mary, and so they united in what you term a betrothal.*

A: Very good, did they continue to have a family?

J: *This is something we do not wish to convey at this time, this shall be revealed.*

A: Wonderful, thank you. So, speaking about Jesus, why is it that there are so many branches of Christianity?

J: *For man has manipulated THE WORD, and there is much darkness in many churches which should be there to be the light. It has been a manipulation of THE WORD, as Jesus stepped away from Judaism the way it had been practiced, and secluded himself with his disciples, and travelled spreading THE WORD, from the group called Essenes. Jesus did not wish to be in areas that gave misinformation.*

So many churches wish to what you term "put a slant" on those words, for not all words are being conveyed. There are many books that have not been incorporated into what you term your "Bible", but it is what it is. Many will find out who or what they are, that they are beings of light from their God Source, and when they do, they will see that like Jesus, He no longer needed a dome, a solid building around Him to house His words.

He roamed freely, did He not? Gathering many crowds on the hills and under the trees? So, we say one does not need a building, a structure, or to pay a tithe or a tax to an institution, to hear my cousin's words, for His words are free to every human being on this Earth plane domain.

When they are activated, when their God Code is opened, they will have direct communion, and there will no longer be a necessity for an edifice called a church. However, there will be edifices and buildings for those who wish to gather together, and celebrate the joy of the wisdom and knowledge that those words bring to them, for not all churches are bad or good, and it is for each person as we spoke about in our last session, intuition, gut — go with what feeds them.

A: Wonderful. I know you already discussed a lot of things. Is there anything you want to tell humanity at this time?

J: *There will be many that will be changed from watching this particular session. Alba we know we have asked much of you and much of this one. We have requested that there be 12 sessions. The reason we asked for 12 was we wished for each one to honour a disciple, for there are many of those disciples living in this present space and timeline. There are three in particular that have not been activated, however when they hear these words, a renaissance will be felt, and immense power and light will transmit from their portals of light.*

You and this one will be reunited as of old because it will be your tribe coming back together to finish the work, for ascension is near. This one is now trumpeting to the people of Earth.

This is an address to the leaders of this Earth planet:

We wish you to look at your nation.
We wish you to look at your people.
How do they fare?
Are they being fed?
Are they being watered?
Are they being sheltered?

As we transmit this message it is the year 2020, and will another year pass by where there are those under your watch

that go homeless, or that go hungry?

And yet you squabble amongst each other looking for control.

You spend what you term "trillions" of money killing each other, warfare, borders, and now you are trying to escape Earth into what you term "the new frontier", and go into space. And yet you haven't conquered famine and homelessness on your Earth plane.

We would like to say, "Clean up your backyard before you try and venture into ours."

Alba, this address will reach many. This one in the future will be talking to leaders of nations, for we will be giving her the information that they need, in order to calm the chaos.

A: Very good, thank you so much. May I ask who I'm speaking to today?

J: *Urka.*

A: Thank you very much Urka. Is there anything else, or do you feel that we are complete today?

J: *Alba, we have a request.*

A: Yes.

J: *We are working on a timeline through you with this one. We do know that you have had sessions prior to this, we do know that you have sessions after this one, however, today, we wish this session to be released as soon as possible, for we wish for many to awaken NOW.*

A: Very good, what would you like to call this session?

J: *The Awakening.*

A: Wonderful. Is that all? Are we complete?

J: *We would like to thank you.*

A: Thank you very much, it's a pleasure, as always.

J: *We are complete.*

CHAPTER FOUR (Session 405)

SELF-EXAMINATION

In this hypnosis session Alba guides Jill to the Angelic Realm and then the session continues with a dialogue with a high-level guide with whom they have been working on a special project.

A: As you step through, I want you to tell me the first thing that you see. Where are you?

J: *I'm floating.*

A: So, as you are floating, look around you and tell me what is there. What do you observe?

J: *Lots of lights.*

A: What colours are these lights?

J: *Well, when I came up the lift, each floor was a different colour; the pink and the green and the blue and the indigo, and when I got to the top it was gold.*

A: Beautiful.

J: *It is almost like all these lights from all the layers are mixing, and there are just sparkly lights everywhere, and as I went through the lift, it was a glass lift, looking out at the universe, and I could see all the stars and all the distant planets, and when we got to the seven, they said "this is the seventh heaven."*

A: Beautiful, what is in the seventh heaven? What do we find there?

J: *It is the celestial.*

A: I would like you now to connect with those that are there waiting for you. Who has come for you?

J: (Jill starts laughing and says "Zac.") *The angels are there, and they have white robes on and have huge wings.* (She laughs some more and then says that they are sitting around like they are having a coffee break.) *One is sitting on what looks like a tree stump with his hand under his chin acting the fool. On Earth there is a sculptor called Rodin and it's like The Thinker, and he has his hand on his chin imitating The Thinker, and they are just having a good time, they are just hanging out taking a break.*

A: So, what is it that they want to tell you today?

J: *They are speaking about home, and what it is to have a home. Oh, and now I am getting so sad. Oh, dear. There are so many on Earth that want to go home because they don't have the connection there, and then they show me all the homeless on Earth, who have been abandoned. But those big, big angel wings, they are now spreading them like an albatross, you know those big, big albatross birds?*

A: Yes.

J: *How big they are with their wings spread. So, these angels in the seventh heaven protect the homeless, shelter them with their wings, protect them until they are ready to go home.*

A: When the angels help the humans, how is it that we feel them?

J: *They say that it is like a gentle breeze. They say some get goosebumps, you know, as if they have just got a little chilly.*

A: Yes.

J: *That is their energy, that is their vibration, gently, gently touching.*

A: Is there a way for us humans to call those angels, in order for us to feel those vibrations?

J: *They said change your form. They said there are many on Earth now. Some put their hands together like praying and that is when your form changes. When your hands and arms are straight when you are walking, when you are sitting.*

A: Yes.

J: *But this is you unconsciously bringing it together to a point of stillness* (Jill puts her hands together as if she is praying) *and it is connected, making a line like that* (she demonstrates what it is). *Others are now holding their hands out and up* (she shows her palms facing upwards and outwards with lifted hands) *and as I do this I can feel the energy coming in through, because hands have to be open to receive.*

When they are together like prayer, that is… supplication is the word that they are using. This is more like an asking: please help me, please help me, I'm struggling, this is what is happening in my life. However, this one (and she once again turns her hands over with the palms facing upwards) *is almost saying I am now open to receive, like your will, right?*

A: Yes.

J: (Jill laughs again.) *So, now they are telling me maybe not so much supplication, as in praying, but more of the openness in the receiving because the praying is more contracted; it brings the hands in, and the other is more open. They are saying it is a time for humanity to have a heart-opening. Open up your hearts and let the light in.*

A: Mmm. How can a human open their hearts with so much going on right now?

J: *We want them to look in the mirror. If a human who hears this does not have a mirror, then we suggest that they look in the window and see their reflection, for are they not here? Have they not been given the gift of life?*

A: Yes.

J: *And breath.*

A: Mmm.

J: *For there are many who are losing their breath this day who would very much like to swap positions with them. For when one is about to lose one's last breath, then only does one give true thanks for the breath that one has had.*

A: So, first and foremost, the breath is the most important?

J: *The breath is everything, for if there is no breath there is no life and, Alba, you were talking to this one earlier about masks and being masked, but we say who is behind the masking? Who are truly wearing masks that you cannot see? For you cannot see what they are doing behind their masks. Who are the ones that have asked you to be masked? For it is separating you from each other.*

A: Yes.

J: *It is time in the privacy of your homes for those who are at martial law because of the masks, they need to take some cleansing breaths, but this time, this too shall pass.*

A: It seems like it is taking forever when you are in that situation.

J: *When it is a joyful time it seems to go by in seconds.*

A: Yes.

J: *When it is a heavier time it seems to take much longer, but did we not speak in our last session about the management of time?*

A: Yes.

J: *So, fill your days with small joys and find something that can uplift you daily, for this is what we wish for this time, for the vibrations to be higher. There are those leaders who call themselves leaders amongst you who are setting the tone for a lower vibration, for the lower the vibration the more fear that is agitated, the easier the people are to be ordered and controlled, and did we not say that this is what you term a new world, and it is being ordered.*

A: Yes.

J: *Fear not, for all has been ordained. It is all part of the plan. The light, as we said, is really opening, and the dark is pushing harder, like a last defence. But it is now at a tipping point, and you and this one who is doing this work, have now opened many more.*

We told this one many years ago that her work will be like a ripple on a pond, travelling over the oceans and reaching many, she did not understand what we were talking about, but now her words which are our words are now reaching many and so it is a weigh-in. When you weigh in for a pre-boxing match and they size each other up, this is a time for sizing oneself up. We spoke to you earlier, Alba, today about what one stands for, this is time to take a stand, make a stand.

Each human that is listening to this broadcast, what is it that they actually stand for? They blindly go about their days, filling up on the outside in. They talk about the new dress, the new hairdo, the new pair of shoes, and there is nothing wrong with that per se. However, is it to their detriment or to their advantage?

As they watch that blue box that we discussed earlier, and it is called a television, who named it such? We want you to break those words up; tell-a-vision. What is the vision that they are telling you? How is that when humans watch the blue box and the ice cream advert comes on and then they get up walk over to the freezer and then they suddenly want an ice cream? They do not even realise that they are being programmed.

Then they see the new car, the washing machine, the new pair of shoes, the new holiday, and this is immediately something that they strive for, sometimes beyond their means, but that is OK because the puppet masters have produced a little square piece of plastic, and this is what you humans term a credit card. What happens with a credit card, many are living beyond their means in order to what you term "keep up with the Joneses" so that they do not feel inadequate.

But we say, fill yourself up from the inside out, for your things do not define who you are, but you are now becoming manipulated, marketed, and taught that you are your things. So, Alba, we gave you an example about the shoes. Could you please discuss this?

A: (Alba laughs.) All right. Right now, I am preparing to pack and I'm packing to move somewhere. I found many shoes that I had purchased. Some were brand new, the heels are too high now, too many of them, so there are many that I am getting rid of that I am not going to use, only keeping the ones that are comfortable for me. So, these are the shoes that I need to let go of, things that no longer belong in my life. They do not identify me any longer.

J: *This is a time for freedom and power, when one gives one's things away that are taking up wardrobe space and cupboards space, things and things and more things, and yet there are so many that are homeless, that are hungry.*

One must ask the audience today how they feel within their hearts when they truly give to another, for is this not truly what it is to be human, to share? For how much, and at whose expense does one need? You know, Alba, these humans, these Earthlings on this domain, we see so many of them, and now I am shown the angels in the seventh heaven, watching the humans on the Earth stage, for it is nothing but a human play, it is a show.

They are showing us in the seventh heaven that it is by your actions, for many say many words, but it is the actions that the angels know you by. For your actions speak louder than your words. So, as they scurry along to their jobs that they do not want to be at, for did they not have such a break over Covid with their family to reconnect, to reunite?

But the blue box gives them a different version of life, for it addresses many wants and very few needs. So, how much work would Earthlings have to do if they did not feel inadequate and knew who they were? They would not have to spend their Earth time scurrying around filling themselves up from the outside in so they are acceptable to each other, for where is the authenticity, where is the realness, the humanity?

Alba, can you imagine what would happen to humanity if they cut their workload in half, and they had three pairs of shoes instead of twenty, thirty, or forty pairs of shoes, and they did not have to spend their time buying stuff that they actually and truly do not need? They would then be able to fill themselves up with each other, with laughter, with creativity, with new ideas.

The puppeteers, the marketers, the controllers, have set the system up with what you term the plastic card, the credit card to enslave.

So, we would like to ask every human listening to this today are they truly human or are they slave human? How much do they need, to fill themselves up from the outside before they realise who they are? When they start giving their trappings away, that is when they will be freer; less to think about, to worry about, less to look after.

You know, Alba, this one is talking a lot today, but she has a lot to say on our behalf. She is now shown what you term a television series when they had a tribe that had never travelled on an air bird, an aeroplane, to a city called London. They were an indigenous tribe. They arrived in this big city, and they were given an experience of staying with different families. One of the families was a farmer and the farmer's wife, and because they were a tribe and they were people that lived on the land, staying with the farmer instead of staying in the city gave them great joy.

But what really perturbed them was going into the farmer's house, and seeing lots of plates on a wall (decoration) and lots of things everywhere, lots of cushions everywhere, and the farmer's wife would spend her time vacuuming with this machine that they had never seen before. They were petrified of it, and they asked her what were the eating plates doing on the wall.

Is this not a plate for eating? And why did she have so many plates, and why was she not spending time with her beloved outside on the land? It seemed to them that she purchased things that she had no need of, no practical need, and she put them on the wall

— she didn't even use them — and I think, Alba, that is exactly the message we would like to give today, to demonstrate that example of what it is that we are trying to convey.

A: Wonderful. I have a question that has been rolling around in my mind since you started talking about this, and that is of the young people who we call influencers, and these are those that get on social media and they basically take different pictures of themselves with different clothing, and different places, and most of those pictures are photoshopped; they are not real, they are not really what they look like. How would you like to address that, as we look into the souls of those people?

J: *Well, that is really what we want to ask today. Is that humanity? What have you become?*

Even that you should have a term called influencer. Why would humans need to be influenced to be able to buy something? Have they truly become robotic? Have they become so dissociated from whom they are, that they need another's thoughts to be put into theirs?

Now, those influencers are being paid what you call money to sell somebody's brand. They are marketers, and those that are being influenced look at the influencers as above them, as on a stage watching this amazing life unfurl, but it is not one that fills one up for long. We don't feel aligned with that particular thought pattern.

A: It seems that they are trying to fill themselves with something.

J: *But it is not lasting. They need approval once again from the outside.*

A: Are we teaching our young children that we need to be approved of?

J: *You know, Alba, this one attended many years ago a talk given by someone called Dr Jim Hurtak. At that talk was a guest speaker who put an image on a screen and there was an audible gasp from the audience, for on the screen was a very beautiful baby about eight months old, sitting, and it looked as if this pure baby was covered in tattoos.*

This one looked at that and thought, which parent would cover such purity in tattoos? She was shocked, and then the screen came closer and Alba, all over that baby were images that had been stuck on it and it was branding; Adidas, Nike, Gucci, Armani, Hermes, Starbucks, Converse, everything that you could think of that is being sold to the humans, and that speaker told her audience that at the age of three years old, they are now having anxiety attacks from pre-schoolers, because when they get to their little kindergarten with their little backpacks, if the latest blue box is saying Barney or the dinosaur or Dora the Explorer and if that little child hasn't got the Dora Explorer's backpack or lunch box, she doesn't feel part of the tribe at the age of three. They have been so marketed.

So, humanity has to think what are they doing to their humanness at this stage, that the little human is feeling inadequate and aware of their inadequacy, at the age of three.

What are they setting those children up for the rest of their lives, that you are nothing but a buying machine, and as long as you adhere to the latest advertising campaign, you will be accepted and acceptable?

What is it that humanity is doing to themselves? It is time to switch off the machine.

A: Well, it is a more peaceful world when you do that. I have not watched it for over eleven years and it definitely changed me.

J: *Well, you have been deprogrammed, Alba.*

A: It is kind of hard to be in the normal world once you have done that; it is like you live in your own world.

J: *But, Alba, that is your inner world.*

A: Yes.

J: *So, do we not say to be of this world but in! Go within.*

A: One of the things written in books long before we started this discourse was about humanity and the technology they used; the technology we consider magic now. The magical schools long ago used technology and vibrations and things like that. Can you talk about that, today? Because I witnessed something that was very magical, and I would like to talk to you about that for a moment. A man had an instrument. He was making sounds with it, musical sounds, and he said he was bringing forth the angels in order to heal with those sounds. As I listened to the sounds he was making and the chanting, every hair on my body was tingling, standing up, and I had vibrations from head to toe. These vibrations, this technology that was used before, can it be used again?

J: *When you learn to disengage from that which is artificial, the artificial stimulation of the blue box, which is a control box, for you are all magical, for you are made of your photonic structure, of light, frequency, sound, creating matter, so that sound and vibration was mixed and the sound was emitted, and you felt the vibration.*

A: Yes.

J: *Your structure reacted to that. So, can you then tell me, Alba, why is it that everyone watching the blue box is not getting that same feeling, because they are disconnected.*

So, in ancient days, many rocks were lifted into places of great weight through a vibrational tuning fork. Humanity have forgotten these techniques, and these techniques, true technology of the gods, that came through the gods, through the human form, into what the gods formed, which was this Earth plane, and they placed their structures, many with hands (Jill starts demonstrating the movements of hands, a particular pattern) *changing the vibrational patterns as we have taught this one, to be a great healer with her hands, with the structures, with the divine patterns, this has been a lost art.*

Alba, we wish for you to work with your frequencies. We are aware of the other work that you are doing; we encourage this.

A: Thank you. I have a question about those rocks. When I was in Peru, for the first time in my life I placed my hands on rocks, and was able to see through the eyes of the rocks. Can you tell me about the consciousness of the rocks?

J: *Alba, everything is frequency. A tree is frequency, water is frequency, light is frequency. Rocks, stones, flowers, everything has frequency. This one that you are talking to today, when she was a little girl, she was able to physically see frequency. She would see it around buildings, she would see it around people, she would see it around plants, and she termed it God's glory.*

She was not incorrect, for your frequency has lifted, your photonic structure has changed, and so you are being able to meld more with nature, you are able to read the energy. So, by placing your hands on the rocks, you were able to tap into that timeline and literally read the rock's story, for everything holds a story.

This one when she was in Peru with you, something made her put her hands on those big rocks, and as she did, they parted, and they unfolded a bit of their story. At the top with all the stairs ascending up was the high priest, with his Sun God rays head-dress on, and his chest pieces, and he beckoned her, come, come and join us for the ceremony, but then she was stopped, because to her left was Sabrina. Sabrina had her hands on the rocks and said, "Do you hear the drums, do you hear the drums?" So, you were all going into that timeline (of nature).

Alba, we see your great love of trees.

A: Yes.

J: *Trees hold much wisdom for you, for when you are tired, we ask for you to sit next to a tree, put your back next to the tree's back as an alignment, like a supplication, like a greeting, and let its warmth, friendship, and its knowledge come to you, for were you not a Sasquatch?*

A: (Alba starts laughing.) Yes (and then she laughs some more.)

J: *This was a happy home for you, and you lived with nature and nature lived with you. You had very big feet, and you were well-grounded and that is why you bring through that groundedness in this current life, and when we said we were turning up your volume, the volume that we are giving you is to teach others how to ground themselves, for your messages through this one, and many others on your platform, will be giving them your Sasquatch feet.*

A: Well, right now I am feeling a great yearning to be around trees. It is more than a yearning; it is like I have to be there.

J: *There is a special spot for you, Alba, and this one tree, in particular, has very big branches. This tree is going to be giving you great comfort, it is waiting for you to come home.*

A: Well, I will need some help in finding it; it's a big country.

J: *It is already in process, Alba.*

A: Yes.

J: *Trust the process.*

A: Thanks, wonderful. So, one of the things that is happening here is that there is a lot of unrest, and we were talking about what makes your blood boil, and what can we do now to ground these people whose blood is boiling.

J: *We take you back to the breath work, and we taught this one a word, and we wrote it across the sky on a clear blue day. It said JOY and you know, Alba, this one has great cheek. She said to us, "Huh. Joy. That is pretty pathetic. Is that the best you can do?" and so we replied, "Just own yourself."*

There are many at the moment that want to put their noses in other people's business, and they are righteous, very self-righteous, for this mask-wearing has created fear in many, and the mask wearers do not wish those that do not wish to wear the masks to be able to have the freedom to choose, for they fear that their very lives are at stake. But those who are choosing not to wear the masks are feeling like their lives are at stake if they do wear the mask.

A: Yes.

J: *For they feel they cannot breathe. So, who is right and who is wrong? Neither, for both are looking at it from their point of view. We taught this one in areas of conflict to please be like a bird, and have a bird's eye view, to rise above the situation to be able to see both sides.*

For how does a mask-wearer understand the freedom and the power that the one that does not have the mask wishes to be free, and the one that does not want to wear the mask, because they are free, cannot understand how the other one wants to be fettered.

So, you have temperatures that rise, and as temperatures rise you have what is termed "the blood is boiling."

A: Yes.

J: *So, one has to look at the situation to find out WHY the blood is boiling, and we say any situation on Earth when your blood is boiling, it is because you are no longer in control.*

The human does not like to not be in control. Unfortunately at this time this mask-wearing and not-mask-wearing are leading to much bigger problems, because underneath the surface the temperature is being turned up, and the boiling is growing and growing and, as a result, issues that were non-issues before, are now becoming big issues, and this is when we spoke about the violence.

Domestic violence has been increasing during this period, because of the frustrations of being locked up. They call it a lockdown, but it is a lock-up, it is a jailing, a closing in. When it should be a time for expansion, it is contraction.

So, neither party is right or wrong, so what we wish to say is "just own yourself." Be as calm as you can be during this time. If you have to wear the mask due to the martial law, do it when you only have to, and then breathe freely in the confines of your own home. When you are calm, your vibration, your frequency will spread like ripples on a pond and, Alba, that is why we wish for you to use your machine.

A: Thank you.

J: *For this will help many.*

A: Yes, thank you so much for that. You know I have been doing these gatherings, putting the people together so we can spread our light. I know that together we can raise our frequency by just having a few people doing that. From your point of view, your higher point of view, right now we are not even allowed to congregate, so what would you like to tell those that know this? They know that if we gather together, we can make a change, make an impact on the world.

J: *Vibrations come from the seventh heaven to many and yet you do not see them. They gather you under their angel wings, so there is a gathering. The gatherings that you have in place, Alba, have affected many. You have what you term a Zoom.*

A: Yes.

J: *Whether they are in person or whether they are online, they will feel the energy. It is better for humanity to be close to each other; their frequency gives off a little spark, a little buzz to each other. That is why they have been missing their hugs so much because, like the tree that we spoke to you about, when you are going to be with that tree, and you will get filled up, like the hug, like the human contact fills them up. However, in the interim, they need to be online. Alba, if you have the time or the capacity, speak to your team, your time manager, to see if you can create more Zooms.*

A: You know, you spoke about the frequencies. I would like to speak about disease and how our belief system causes disease.

How does that work?

J: *This one many years ago had what you termed a skiing accident. It was severe. We instigated that accident, for her energy was everywhere, discombobulated, and we needed her to do work for us.*

But while she still had her two legs, she was all over the show. We told her if she did not slow down, we would take her out, so on the first day of a new ski season she helped another soul on the slopes, and we gave her the freedom of what it felt like to fly. She came down that ski field faster than she had ever skied and she truly felt like she was flying.

Her one ski hit a tiny pocket of snow and that ski touched her forehead and it went snap, snap, crack, crack, crack. We did major damage, for we needed for her to be quiet for quite a while.

When she went for her MRI, she never usually listened to breakfast radio, but because she had an early appointment her husband took their children to school that day, and when she listened, the radio announcer said if you ever go for an MRI and they ask you if you want music, say no because they put the headphones on and then the music goes la, la, la, and then suddenly the MRI starts and it goes ba, ba, ba, ba, ba and then la, la, la. We actually wanted this one to hear no music that day, for we wanted to make one of our first appearances.

As she was lying on that MRI table, this one who has never been a religious person, still cannot get her head around your last session, said to the All That Is, "Thank you for creating a human being that designed this machine, for without this machine, if this had happened three hundred years ago, I would not know the damage to my leg, and I might never walk again."

With her gratitude, she then said, for she has a very inquiring mind, "I wonder how this machine works." So, we showed her a graph with resonance image and a magnet that brought it together of a fish finder, and she said in her mind, "Oh, MRI. Magnetic resonance, which creates an image." Then, to deepen this one's experience, we travelled with her at that moment to a place on Earth that you term Stonehenge.

We got her to move between the stones. If there were two short stones together it made a short "boing, boing" sound. If it was wider apart then she went "booooiiinnngg, boooiiiinnng" and we told her, "This is resonance. This is frequency. This is vibration."

Stonehenge used to be a receiving and a transmitting station, and that is how the ancients, when she was one of the ancients, spoke to the gods, through the resonance and the vibration of the way they erected those stones, with their tuning forks.

We then explained to this one about the energy of the human body. So, today, Alba, with your permission, we would like to teach humanity how their systems work.

A: Wonderful, thank you.

J: *OK, so we showed this one fine white mist coming into the human mouth. We said, "You can give this many names; prana, life force, blessing, spirit, oxygen. Name it whatever you would like. This mouth that every human has, where they get their breath, we want them to think about the mouth as the lobby of their hotel (their body is their hotel) and in their hotel, they have seven floors and, on each floor, they have a lift door.*

As they breathe in, it goes through their lobby to their lift door, it runs up and down their lift shaft, from the top of the crown to the base of their toes, and instantly there is a vortex or a portal for an energy transfer system, and as the energy (breath) hits it, each lift door opens at exactly the same time in the nano, (she makes the sound it makes) *phew, phew, phew, very fast.*

It goes through the blood, it goes through the tissue, the veins, the bones. Everything that is there, but, Alba, men have emotions, and this is when we come to the disease — the dis-ease — and the belief systems.

So, we showed this one how many men, not women but many men, hold their anger, their blood boiling, their rage, in their chests. Alba, have you not heard the term "red with rage?"

A: Yes.

J: *Emotions have colour, and this is where the disease comes in, the belief of disease which is just a belief within them, within oneself. So, the red with rage is now dense because colour is dense. So, instead of that breath and that energy going into and through that entire chest cavity, and feeding and energising all the cell structures, it now has a blockage so only a little can go through, go past the gatekeeper they put in themselves.*

Now that part is no longer at ease; it is now at dis-ease, and so the cells malform, they malfunction. They change their photonic structure, it changes. It can now become what you term cancer, or a heart attack, a blockage.

But it is self-inflicted. Once again, lack of control through the belief system that they have to be a certain way. As a result, their body is no longer at ease, it is now at dis-ease and then it becomes diseased through that belief system. We then showed this one when it comes in, whether you are male or female, no matter your nationality, child, adult, no matter what religion you are, you come from source. You have the breath of source. It is pure, but what is it going to be when it comes out of your mouthpiece, as you speak to those around you? Will you bless them, or do your words poison them?

As we said in the last session, whatever you give out is what you choose to come back to yourself. So, there is no surprise that when one gossips about another, which is only because there is lack within self, then that gossip will come back.

What is it that you choose, what is your belief system, what dis-ease do you choose for yourself? Know thyself, be true to thyself. Does that answer your question?

A: Yes. So, as we continue along that same subject as you use frequencies on these people, whether it be reiki or whether it be any other type of frequency, how does that help those diseased cells? Does it remind them of what they are?

J: *We had a conversation with this one yesterday when she met a person who is on her awakening, and this person told her that her hands were doing funny things, and this one told her that when we taught her to do the healing with her hands, that this hand* (Jill indicates her left hand), *had to hold the energy and vibration in place, for this hand was doing the changes of the photonic structure, and the vibration and the frequency. For if she moved this hand away, that vibrational photonic structure would be like a drop in the ocean, as opposed to a drop in a teacup.*

We wanted it to be strong energy, and that was a blockage, that was a colour, that was a gatekeeper holding the energy in place like a laser beam.

So, because you are nothing but vibrations of light, by your very light "being," each and every one of you are able to not only heal yourself, heal your thought, heal your body, but you are able to change the photonic structure of another.

A: Beautiful, wonderful, thank you so much. Is there anything else that you have for us today, or do you feel we are complete for today?

J: *Alba, today I feel that we are complete. I feel that this session is a lot for humans to take in.*

A: Yes.

J: *There was a lot for them to think about, and we would prefer it to be concise today.*

A: Wonderful. What would you like to call this session today?

J: *Self-examination.*

A: Wonderful. Do you have any parting words for humanity at this time?

J: *Humanity now needs to breathe. For much of their breath has been sabotaged.*

(Jill then coveres her mouth and her words are muffled.)

When one talks like this now, one's words are muffled, and when one removes it one can hear. We wish for many now to do some self-examination, some self-care. Long baths, as water is a healer. Spend time in nature when allowed, deep breaths, calming music and, of course, Alba, a Zoom session with our Queen of Frequency, Alba.

A: (Alba starts laughing.)

J: *Thank you very much for that.*

CHAPTER FIVE (Session 408)

PEACE FOR THE WORLD

In this hypnosis session Jill goes to a meeting in the Galactic Hall, where beings are watching what's unfolding on planet Earth. The session continues with a guide with whom they have been working on a special project. They discuss how we are designing our lives with our thoughts and the power of words. They speak of truth, peace, the resurrection, and the Awakening.

A: I'd like for you to describe to me what it is that you're seeing right now.

J: *A very large screen.*

A: A very large screen. Where is this screen?

J: *It's inside the spaceship. There are panels of windows all around me and I can see planets as we pass them. We're driving at hyper speed and it's like* Star Wars *where you see streaks of light as we are travelling so fast. I'm being told it is like being in a worm-hole, and you're just shooting through space, and I can now see outside the spacecraft.*

Although I'm inside the spacecraft, I can also view it from the outside. It looks really small as it travels through this enormous tunnel — this wormhole. These wormholes carry you, when you get inside them, your vehicle can travel immense distances and immense speed, and that's how we travel intergalactic.

A: And where is it that you're going today? Where is this ship taking you?

J: *We've got a meeting; we're going to The Great Hall.*

A: Wonderful. Tell me when you get there.

J: *Well, my spaceship is docking. I've got a very large fleet behind me, they're escorting me. They have escorted me, and I've got a long cloak on behind me. You know like the Queen of England and her ermine coat, and it goes all the way down to the ground. Well, mine is gossamer thin and it's trailing behind me. I'm incredibly tall, I've got very long, long, long limbs. I've got three fingers and I'm well, I wouldn't say crystalline, but I'm glowing.*

I'm just glowing, the others are waiting for me because we have a council meeting in The Great Hall, and they've come from all over the galaxy today. Actually, it's evening time; although there's no time, it's like twilight. They are emissaries, travelling in from their planets, from deep in the galaxy. This is the triad that we were speaking of in an earlier session.

We are now in The Great Hall. We are assembling and there's a projection, we are in a semi-circle and we are in, umm... although we're in chairs, they are floating and the tables are floating, and we are all looking ahead onto a big projection, and we're looking at the trouble from the other area of our galaxy, those rogues, the rogue element, those ones trying to slip through the portals and the trap doors.

At the same time, there's another screen playing of Earth, and everything that's unfolding on Earth, but we have sent a collective energy from deep within the galaxy that is on its way to Earth because, as we said, this is a war for the souls of humanity for ascension.

Luckily, we can see the rogues at the same time as we can see Earth, so we can see where the infiltration is taking place, and we know that by sending this energy that's coming to Earth, it is going to lift and change the photonic structure of everyone on the planet, and that is what you call "having an ace up your sleeve."

We've spoken about what happens when people awaken, what happens when they get the photonic structure downloads which lifts the vibrations, we said disruptions. In the very first session with this one we spoke about a destabilisation in order to stabilise, and this is what we were talking about, for when people have the vibration, the frequency to higher knowledge, they can see the puppeteers, they can see the game that is being played, then humanity will gain an upper hand.

This is the disruption that is coming in. It's coming from the rogue element that is trying very hard to stop the collective of humanity rising to a greater and a higher consciousness, and that is why they are implementing the protests.

This is why the economies are shutting down; they are trying to put the people into a state of fear, for when the people are in a state of fear, they then close themselves off to anything larger, anything out there, and they put themselves into survival mode, and their energies decrease.

But when a nation is housed, when a nation is not hungry, when a nation has jobs, warmth, food, and security, then a nation has time to think, and the puppeteers do not wish the slave human to have time to think.

Too many were waking up, they've been watching your airwaves, your Internet, your social media, and they are shutting down what you term lots of sites that talk about freedom and truth, for they do not wish this to reach the populace, for the more that are awake, the less grip they hold.

A: For those of us who are awake, it almost seems as if them shutting everything down is actually waking more people up.

J: *Well, we spoke about truth and conspiracy, and there are those that are asleep, that accuse those that are awake of conspiracy, and this is how the puppeteers have controlled for aeons. We need to reach many more, for there are too many platforms that are being denied.*

A: I'd like to talk a little bit more about this wave that's coming in. Where is this wave coming from? I've heard that the sun has been emitting a lot of energy for some that are very sensitive that can hardly sleep from all of the energy. Is this the energy you speak of, or is it something different?

J: *No, this is not the energy from the great central sun. This is fusion — fusonic energy nebulae, deep within the galaxy. This is an energy you have not experienced before on Earth. With this energy, it will create not only internal disruptions but external disruptions.*

A: When you speak of disruptions, sometimes people feel that it's negative. What will these disruptions be? Are they planetary disruptions, are they mental disruptions?

J: *We are showing this one the image of a married couple, and when they have an argument, the argument is not pleasant. However, the issues that the argument brings to the surface are what makes that relationship healthy, for they are no longer hidden, they are not internal; they do not make the human bodies ill, and it bubbles to the surface, and so it is with a physical eruption.*

Many will see this as negative; many will see this as disruptive and destructive. However, what it will do for humanity, it will bring humanity back together, it will give humanity a common cause, it will unite humanity as one.

For all class distinctions, those who felt superior, those who felt inferior, will be equal. It will be the great leveller, and many systems will change because of this. The bondage that you've lived under will fall away, and a new way of being and a new way of trading and a new way of bartering will take place.

Humanity will hear themselves, their sweetness of being will be there, displayed in a new way. This will be what is termed the golden era.

A: Is this golden era soon upon us?

J: *Earthlings love timelines. They live for time, but we would like to say that this is going to happen in a timely fashion.*

A: Okay, very good. We spoke about trust, and I know that these questions you gave us today were very important, and one of the questions I'd like to go through is a song that you brought up. That song was written by Cat Stevens and, it's *The Peace Train* and you had said that music is a balm to the soul, for it rests it, and we wish for you to study the words. (Alba reads out what Jill had sent her that morning from her guides.)

Peace, there was a song about a peace train and the one who wrote it is a master of his time. We wish humanity to look upon those words, for those words are more important today than ever before.

So, *The Peace Train.*

Now, I've been happy lately
Thinking about the good things to come
And I believe it could be
Something good has begun

Oh, I've been smiling lately
Dreaming about the world as one
And I believe it could be
Someday it's going to come

Cause out of the edge of darkness
There rides the Peace Train
Oh, Peace Train take this country
Come take me home again

And it continues by saying…

Get your bags together,
Go bring your good friends, too

Cause it's getting nearer,
It soon will be with you

Now come and join the living,
It's not so far from you
And it's getting nearer,
Soon it will all be true

Now I've been crying lately,
Thinking' about the world as it is
Why must we go on hating,
Why can't we live in bliss?

Cause out on the edge of darkness,
There rides a Peace Train
Oh, Peace Train take this country,
Come take me home again

So, can you tell me a little bit about these words and why you wanted to bring this to our attention?

J: *Well, we chose these words because they depict everything that humanity needs to concentrate on at this time. People love to climb aboard a new cause, a new process, and this time we would like them to climb on board the peace train.*

For war serves no one, no-thing, no country, and this peace train is the train that drives one, that one has peace inside one's train, one's train of thoughts.

Is one's train of thoughts at peace or at war, internally? And with the quickening upon us, and the quickening is the energy that is arriving. And we said once before, when it hits it is like a wave.

For some, it will be a wild ride, and for others, it will be gentle. But if they are on board the peace train, they will have a gentle ride, a gentle experience, and as they hold their stillness and their peace, it will emanate to another.

For, Alba, for the people you know in your life, those who are solid, who are quiet, who know who they are, who have a stillness, do you not find comfort there?

A: Yes.

J: *For they are at peace. For the more people that get on board the peace train now, it will make it a smoother ride, and a smoother transition for many.*

A: Wonderful, wonderful, thank you so much. It reminds me of 1992 when we had a major hurricane in Florida, and it was devastating. Many people lost their homes, many were jobless, and our home seemed to have been magically just rattled a little bit. It was as if the whole world around us, everything around us was devastated except for our little area, where nothing happened, and I often wondered, how could that be? It was almost like the hands of God were around our neighbourhood. So, when you're in the peace train, when you're riding the peace train, is that what it's like?

J: *You cause your own protection. You cause your own experience, by the lowering of one's vibrations, or the rising of it above.*

For if one can be on top of the wave, rather than caught in the breaking down of it as it hits the shore, would not the experience be different?

A: It sure would, yes. Thank you.

J: *So, why does one wish to be caught in the turbulence? Rather, be rising above the situation, floating on the energy, floating on the jet stream. And lifting you where you need to go and settle.*

A: Wonderful, thank you. One of the questions that you had given us is what life are you designing, building, creating for self? So, if these times that are coming are so turbulent, can you please explain what that question is about?

J: ***Well, the question that we really wanted to get humanity to think about today, is who do they live for?***

We've said this before but now we have termed it in a different way as to how they are designing their homes. And when we talk about their homes, we're talking about this home, an internal home, this external home, this 3D matter, this internal body of light, for they are light travellers.

They are energetic beings having a human experience and yet they forget who they are, and they think they are 3D flesh, blood, and bones, but that is their coat, that is the dress they put on, that is the covering to get them from A to B. But the actual existence, the experiences in this current incarnation should be directed by themselves.

However, so many play the victim, play the blame game, because they do not stand in their own power.

They do not take self-responsibility, responsibility for this self. And when they do that, it is like standing in a stagnant pool and going nowhere. We want flow. We have free will in the universe, we have free will on this Earth plane and yet people have forgotten they have free will. But it is the fear that holds the human back.

Alba, many stay in relationships because of what is termed "financial security." If you bestowed what you term "money" onto many people, and there was no fear of a lack of a home, lack of warmth, lack of financial security, then there would be many, many, many, thousands if not millions designing and living a different life for themselves.

But we would like honesty and truth. We want these to look at the mirror to see what they see. What is looking back at them?

Is this a brave soul? Is this a soul that is blaming another for the lack in their life?

It is all about choices, you design the life for yourself through your choices, and the time is coming when choices need to be made.

We said to this one, and she did a reading for somebody yesterday, and we spoke about being clear as crystal, for did she not say that she is trumpeting, and the trumpets are near? For when you stand in something that is similar to The Great Hall and you have your interview, which is termed your "end of life exit" through your way-station, what is it that you will say at your interview?

How did you live your life? How was your current incarnation? What excuses will you give before your wise ones? For they read your soul.

And now it is a time for soul reading, for when all are clear and crystal, one can move forward into any situation, and so it is a time, as we said in our last session, for self-examination, examination of the self.

Just own yourself.

A: You also spoke about what is it that is toxic in your life. Would that be part of this?

J: *Correct, Alba.*

A: What does that do when you are toxic in your life?

J: *This is when you are poisoning yourself with your thoughts by doing the blame game. You are throwing what is termed a "pity party", and your friends, who do not have the strength to let you know that throwing a pity party is just treading water.*

This one threw beautiful pity parties, she was a professional pity party thrower, and yet when she was going through it, she did not see it, but when we changed her photonic structure and she saw it for what it was, she couldn't stop laughing and she couldn't believe the amount of time she had wasted.

So, the toxicity is anything that causes an uncomfortable spot in the body.

For if anyone is having aches or pains, discomfort, dis-ease, disease from a belief system, it is caused by an underlying current of toxicity.

So, this is why we want truth seekers to be a truth seeker. When they look in the mirror, Alba, we want them to imagine it as a magic mirror that can see right through them. No deceit, no deceit for self.

You know, in other planets, Alba, we do not have this problem, for one can instantly read another's thoughts, there is nothing to hide, so it is nothing but truth and expansion.

That is what we wish for those who are listening here today, to imagine that everything that they think or say about another internally, or say especially about themselves, can be seen and heard by all. Would they then change their thinking? We think so.

A: Yes, I think so. Can you talk to me about power, and how we have given away and released our power?

J: *When you have toxic thoughts, when you have disease in the body, you have released your power. You've given it away. For this self is your energetic house, your energetic centre.*

You have electricity stations on your Earth plane that provide energy. Your form is your powerhouse, this is your power station, and every time that you give a little away by not being true to yourself you diminish your power. And so, we would like to give you an example.

If all Earthlings get $100 of power to run their systems daily — woman, child, man, all Earthlings, and every time they have a negative thought about self or of another, that energy goes down $95, $90, $80, $60.

How much have they depleted their power base by the end of the day? Are they in deficit or are they in credit? How do they choose to live? How do they choose to design that energy centre, that powerhouse, that power station? Every human runs and plugs in their own power base.

Why would they give their power away when the other has been issued the same amount?

A: Well, it seems we've been programmed that way since birth, to give away our power to authority, to others that are in a higher status than us. It seems like it's a program that we have been born into, giving our power away to our spouse, to our family members.

J: ***There is no one that is of higher status than oneself.***

For one is never above and one is never below, one is not to the front and one is not to the back, but one travels side by side, and that is the problem on Earth. One gives status to another when one feels less than another. Doctors, lawyers, professionals, those who are learned do not hold a higher status than the beggar on the street.

This is something that has been programmed for ego and distinction. For have we not said your things do not define who you are, but your essence, your heart? There lies your wealth, there lies your power. For Mother Theresa was one, as we said before, with great essence, and yet she had no wealth.

Jesus had great essence; his wealth was in the love that he had for the people. People need to think about how they're giving their power away to those who they deem to have higher status, and that is why we said there are so many on Earth spending so much time buying things they do not need in order to give them status.

For you have many roaming around in cars, which is a vehicle that will take you from A to B, and one is a Porsche, and a Ferrari, and a Lamborghini, and a Bentley, and a Rolls Royce.

Does not the Mini Minor get you to the same place? Are you not travelling the same distance? Yes, one has more comfort; does this mean that that one that travels in the Bentley is of a higher status? No, it means that they have been programmed more.

We wish to now make a clarification. Not all who have things are trapped, for there are many humans who have immense power of heart and essence who have beautiful things, for they do not see the one that is in the Mini Minor as less than themselves. They do not put them or place them on a lower status, for these are masters who live amongst you.

But there are so many Earthlings that give and erode the power base daily where they have anxiety because they feel they are not enough. They don't meet the standard. They are not acceptable, and so many of these are the alone dwellers. And then you have something that is termed suicide, and the suicide is from many different factors, but the largest factor is not being able to fit in. Not having status, not having the right house, the right school, the right car, the right clothes — right for who or for whom?

And that's why we say who are you living for?

Who are you designing your house for? Your home, your physical home, your 3D home? For you are here, but for a temporary time, a small Earth fragment of time. Do you wish to spend it in anxiety, and fear and lack? Or are you self-contained? Contained in self. So, that is why we say, Alba, know who you are.

You are a spark of light, from the All That Is.

You are a cell in the structure of All That Is.

There is nothing that has not been ordained.

Live in the moment, make this moment count.

For when this moment counts, the next moment will look after itself.

It has not arrived yet, but yet everybody is already living in the future.

Planning in the future that may never come.

So, we would like you all to be a designer of one moment.

A: Beautiful. You spoke to Jill about independence and told her that you needed to split up that word. Can you tell me what that is?

J: *There are many words that we would like humanity to split, for when they split their words and play with their words and the nuances of the words, they will actually understand what that word means, and we told her many years ago, humanity needs to study the meaning of the words that they use, that just flow out of their portal of light.*

This mouthpiece that is speaking to you now is here to teach humanity about their power, the power that comes out of the portal of light. And as she speaks, as she puts her hands now, these fingers in front of her mouth, and she has spoken before, on her group called 4 I Am Universe, to teach people to put their hands in front of their mouths and speak and as they do this, they will feel the vibration of who they are against their fingers.

That is their power.

The most important organ in their body is their portal, is their mouthpiece, for the words that come out hold immense weight. For these words can start wars and these words can create peace throughout nations, for is it not words that all your politicians use, political movements? And so, we come back to the word independence.

Who or what are you dependent on? You all look to the external, but everything is internal. In the silent voice, and in the stillness is when you get the point of creation. That is when you feel your vibration and know who you are. So, when you go into the dependence, and depend on self, and realise that self is aligned with the All That Is, there is no need for external, external anything. For it is all internal, and yet humanity is filling itself up on the external.

You know, Alba, when you seek approval, and we have stated that the only approval that one needs is the approval of self. For when one has self-love, love of the self, then things will flow, you will move out of the stagnant pool. For the All That Is created this energetic form.

So, what are you saying to the All That is when you find fault in this perfect form? Do you say to the All That Is, "You created imperfection, you are not a great designer"?

And yet you're on this Earth plane, and as you walk you have grass, you have flowers, you have air, you have ocean, you have water, you have lakes, you have the sun, you have the moon, you have the clouds and you have the joy of each other, all your playmates. So, how can one see imperfection, not only in self, but in another? You are all playing a part, this is a beautiful stage. What part is it that you wish to play? Go, experiment and have fun. Find the joy, find the joy.

A: Wonderful. If we are this body that we designed, can we redesign it in perfect health?

J: *We can, we would like to point to you as a perfect example; are you not glowing at the moment?*

A: Yes.

J: *Have you not found your joy again?*

A: Yes.

J: *Are not many humans saying, "Look at Alba, look at Alba! She has no wrinkles, her eyes are bright, they are luminous and shining. Her joy is glowing for she is radiating from the inside out." For, Alba, you, after Peru, now know who you truly are.*

You have claimed your power back, and as you have claimed your power back, you are now able to be gentle and kind, for you are now gentle and kind to self. But how can one be gentle and kind to another, if one is not gentle and kind first to oneself? For one can only see in another what one can see in oneself.

So, when one does not see imperfection in self, one will not see imperfection in another, and that is why it is so important to go within and connect with All That Is, to remind oneself that one is nothing but perfection.

A: So, when one thinks of ourselves as perfect, we can heal ourselves. We are perfect.

J: ***The less fault one finds in self, the more they are healed.***

A: Wonderful. I was just listening to a discourse from someone who was talking about a hospital in China in which these masters would chant in their own language, "You are perfect" to an organ that was diseased and, with their chanting and their intention, the actual tumour disappeared. So, just with intention, it seems that we can change the world.

J: *Well, intention is thought, and thought is energy in (energetic form) and that is when one holds a negative emotion, it is held in a cell, and that cell starts to mutate, it starts to change its form, and therefore that cell is no longer at ease, and then it becomes diseased. So, what is one thinking?*

A: So, this cancer that we're creating with thought on Earth right now, this dis-ease, of the mind, of the protests, that are destructive, things like that, those that are here as light-workers, and those that are helping us from other realms, what should we set our intention to? Is it just peace?

J: *Protests can be done peacefully, but remember, for every action, there is a reaction. So, if one is a protestor, demonstrates and protests with immense anger, then one will receive immense anger back.*

For whatever one gives out, one receives back. So, we suggest that you have an old-fashioned term called a sit-in, where there's no anger. It is a discontent; it is a need for change. No abuse being hurled, for then abuse will be hurled back, and that lowers the vibration, and that sits in the cells.

What does one wish to hold in the cells, stagnant or free flowing? We ask, how can it be free flowing when it is full? So, one tips it all out, one has a gentle sit-in, with one's beautiful words of what one wishes to see, for words, as we said, hold weight, words have power. Do you wish to antagonise one, or do you wish, those that are in power, to see powerful words? What does one wish for?

A: Yes, so you spoke about the resurrection. Are we speaking about the resurrection of Earth, or something else?

J: *We are speaking about Yeshua and his resurrection.*

A: Can you tell me about that?

J: *Is he not here now? Are his disciples not doing his work? This is not the resurrection, this is the part of the second coming, and it is a time for people to be resurrected, for what does it mean to be resurrected?*

One is dormant, there is no life in the building; the lights are off. One is now being shown a city in the United States called Detroit, where it was like that city had gone down, and now parts of it are being resurrected, with life coming back, and so the light of the Christ, the Christ light is being resurrected. It is coming. Oh, this one feels it.

It is coming from the nebulae, deep within the galaxy, and this is the light, this is the light within, and it is coming for all, for did He not say, He is the light, all who gather under Him, under His light, will be resurrected?

It is time for resurrection, it is a time for rising, for your Earth plane, incarnation is but for a short period, and then you will go to your home bases.

So, what part are you playing in your own resurrection, in your own ascension? For ascension and resurrection are very aligned, but one cannot ascend if one is not resurrected. What do you choose, Alba? What do they choose?

Do they wish to be the 30kg weight luggage dragging around daily or do they want to be the 7kg in the overhead? As a light traveller, they forget who they are, they are so embroiled in this meat suit. We wish for their light to shine, and unite under the T for trust, which we show, Alba, with the cross of Christ being crucified, and many who are light-workers have undergone a crucifixion, for there are those who are asleep that crucify those who are awake. But Jesus was resurrected, and so shall you.

A: For those that listen, or read these words, who don't believe in Jesus and get offended by talk about the resurrection and the crucifixion, and the fact that they have to be under the light of Christ, how do you address someone like who was brought up in a different religion, or who has completely rejected anything taught by religion? What would you say for those now that are in this point of change?

J: *There is a big difference between what is termed the light, and religion.*

For if they reject the light, they reject self, for they are light particles. Religion is man-made, but the light is eternal.

Energy transforms and reconfigures into different shape and form for different experiences, for different dances. But religion is dogma. But those that have been programmed to live under certain dogma will come into their own, as the wave approaches, as the light approaches, for not only is this light, Christ light, crystalline — that is what Christ is; crystalline — it is clear and there is no fault, for it comes directly from source through Christ.

When we speak of the name Christ, let us change it. Those who prefer a different word for Christ, came for no other reason to make people conscious, as opposed to unconscious.

So, let us now talk about the conscious light, arriving in this Earth domain, for those who feel more comfortable with the words, for as we said before, words hold immense power. So, one would be upset with the word Christ, but could one be offended with the word conscious? And yet it is one and the same.

Do you now understand the importance of the nuance of the word?

Did that explain what it is you wish to know?

A: Yes, thank you very much. You had spoken that it is time to be like oil and water. Is that like being on top of the water that you had spoken about before, or is it different?

J: *It is floating on top, being part of, but not getting involved with the things, the lurking below. Alba, we wanted to tell you about how we used this vessel to actually clean up the oil on the water. And so, we set it in motion and the reason that we are explaining this story at this time, for we want to show the Earthlings the power of who they are, for they see themselves as 3D, and yet we wish them to see themselves in a much broader sense.*

In the year 2010, Dominus (one of Jill's guides) *spoke to this one for the first time on a winter's day; she thought she was having a stroke. You experienced her talking in Peru, chatting to us, and in 2010 this happened to her for the very first time, and yet we spoke to her then in an ancient Aramaic language from her home base.*

We told her it was Dominus, Lord Protector, Lord Galactor, Lord Almighty we to bow unto and before him.

That is when we spoke to her about the discourse, and we said let the discourse begin, that she was a channel, she needed to open up and let the light in.

After that discourse that we had with her, she was working as a real estate agent, and every time she had a buyer or a seller, she gave them a present in gratitude, but there was one particular house that we put the circumstances together, that she would not be able to buy that buyer a present, and we waited two years for the perfect strategy to play out.

We spoke to her on that winter's day, and two weeks later she passed by the house and she saw a car in the driveway, and she knocked on the door and she met a being, an ascended master, who was staying at the house, who was friends of the owners, and she said please, can she drop off a present, and the lady said yes.

She came back, and she dropped off her present, and the lady gave her her business card. On the business card there was a double tetrahedron, and there were rainbow colours, and this one thought, "That's odd. That looks what is termed "new age spiritual", and she said to the person, "Oh, what does this mean?" And the ascended master said, "Why, it is a double tetrahedron."

On the Monday, the ascended master called her and said, "Could I please meet you for lunch?" And this one was terribly busy, but we made sure that she met her for lunch, and they sat at a restaurant, and the ascended master said to her, "I have a message for you. Could you please come back to the house?" This one thought that was odd because if the buyers were saying thank you for the present, why can't this lady just say it there instead of taking her back to the house, and this lady knew nothing about this one other than knowing that she was a real estate agent.

She was taken back to the house and she was put on the kitchen chair, and the ascended master said, "I feel like I have to close my eyes now." The ascended master opened her mouth and started speaking to this one in the same language that we had spoken to this one two weeks prior.

This one thought she may have been on candid camera, that somebody was trying to play a joke. She opened one of her eyes to peek, but there was nothing there. This ascended master said to her, "They are here, do you understand?"

This one then understood that those that had spoken to her two weeks prior were now present, and then this one felt a pyramid just above her belly button, but it was shaped like a funnel.

The ascended master then said to her, "Is the pyramid in place?" And this one had never experienced anything as bizarre. She thought, what on earth is going on here? and she said, "Yes, the pyramid is in place."

Then the ascended master said to her, "They are requesting to use your body as a vessel to clear up the ocean." That there had been a huge oil spill, oil everywhere, damaging your Earth plane, and they would like to use her vessel. She thought it was ridiculous, that her Jill, a little 3D, was being asked by these supreme beings to clean up the ocean. So, she very facetiously said, "Yep, sure, no problem."

She was then asked to ground herself and she'd heard of the word grounding but she didn't know what that meant. So, she said to the one guide that she knew, "Aurelius if you want me to ground myself, you better do it or show me because I don't know what it really means." She was on the Earth and she travelled through the Earth, and she saw fire, molten fire, and then she travelled further, and we took her to the centre of the Earth, and she was in the most enormous cavern, and she heard drip, drip, drip, and that was the heartbeat of Gaia.

And she had water, and she had fire, and she came out of the Earth, and she shot through, and she hit the air, and so she was grounded. So, the ascended master started working round her, doing what was necessary to clean up the Earth and take it through this one, through the portal, to the All That Is, to clean up what the greed of humanity had done to this beautiful, beautiful Earth plane, and we thanked her.

She did not know what she had done, and yet we required the power of who she is, not the 3D, for she did not see herself in all that she was, and we give you this example today, for the Earthlings that walk amongst you, that they have incredible power to make radical changes to this Earth plane, to clean the air, to assist climate change, for they, united, with intention, are very powerful beings.

This one went to work the next day, Alba, and the secretary said to her, "Did you listen to the TV breakfast show this morning with the breaking news?" It was about the oil spill in the Gulf of Mexico, and she said "no," and they said, "The scientist has said there must have been an organism that ate up all the oil overnight, for it has mostly dissipated," and yet it was this one, with the power from the All That Is that had cleared it.

And that is why we wish to speak repeatedly of power, Alba. You are all-powerful beings. It is time to claim your power and your sovereignty.

A: Wonderful, thank you. So, all of the questions have been answered today except for one, which is Bob Marley's song, One Love. Why have you brought that to Jill's attention?

J: *Alba, I think we have held a sufficient discourse today, and as you see your computer battery's at 80%. You've given away 20% of your power. Alba, one love is what this Earth is all about. There is one, there are many but there is one, all from the same source and yet they fight amongst themselves when it should be brought together as "one love."*

As we spoke about the peace train, all Earthlings who listen to this, if they put on the song The Peace Train *and then they play the song* One Love *those vibrations that emanate from those songs will sit within their structures, and they will find contentment.*

It will settle them; it will settle their nerves. For if you go to a party on Earth, Alba, and you play heavy metal, does it not give you a different feeling and a different resonance as if you had to play Peace Train*?*

A: Yes.

J: *It is time for changing the dissonance and the resonance.*

A: Wonderful. Thank you so much. Is there anything else, or do you feel that we are complete for today?

J: *We would like to thank you once again for your patience, Alba. We see you working in all that you do with your teachings with Antonio, with your brother of light, and those that you are training to do the work that you do. We commend you for that. We see you doing many other hypnosis sessions. Soon, when all is settled and dis-settled and dispersed, and there's travel again on your Earth plane, your work will change, but for now we see the load you carry. We ask you please to ask for assistance, for you need rest, for the time ahead will be a busy time.*

A: Wonderful, thank you. What will we call this discourse for today?

J: *Peace for the world.*

A: Peace over the world?

J: *Peace for the world.*

A: Thank you, it's a good name for a chapter. Thank you so much. Are we speaking with Urka today or somebody else?

J: *No, you are speaking with Uriel, she* (Jill) *is a fractal of Uriel; this is the light coming through.*

A: Wonderful, anything else, or are we done today?

J: *The galactic federation is aligned. They are ready with the other, the triad is strong, The Great Hall had a celebration, Alba. This one, our ambassador, from the Intergalactic Federation of Light, is working on her mission.*

She sits with Jesus, with Yeshua, on that council, part of the triad.

That Christed light, that consciousness for those who do not like the word Christ, is nearing.

Those who are awake are feeling it; there is a tiredness in humanity at the moment. Not only from the stress that the Covid has caused, but the energetic waves that are coming in — they are changing the photonic structure, for the Mini Minor motors will no longer run the Lamborghini energy.

But this is the time of awakening, this is the time of ascension, this is a time for the designing of self, for it is a resurrection, it is saying goodbye to the old life and celebrating new life. We wish you well. So be it.

A: Thank you very much.

CHAPTER SIX (Session 412)

BALANCE

In this hypnosis session Jill goes to the planet Aurora where she is queen and teaches the beings of that planet about creation. Her guides talk to us about Shekinah, the power of words and emotions, and the need for balance in preparation for the great leveller.

A: What do you notice?

J: *I'm a queen, I'm actually in charge of Aurora.*

A: Tell me about Aurora.

J: *It's crystalline and it has vegetation all around it, and it is protected. It is a light-filled planet, it has many, many, waterfalls, and the beings are peaceful.*

A: What do the beings look like on this planet?

J: *They're very tall, their skin is like a lizard. My eyes are very, very, large, and they have yellow flecks.*

A: What's the shape of your eyes?

J: *Sort of like a crocodile. I've got bumps on my head, similar to the term afro, Afro-American corns.* (Jill demonstrates how the hair is braided on the head, one in the middle and on each side of the head).

A: The corn rows on the hair.

J: *Yes, there are three. My ears are flat. Flat ears, narrow face, highly intelligent, highly telepathic.*

A: What does your body look like?

J: *I have a stumpy tail; I've got long feet with claws on the end. Very, very, strong thighs and shins, long and sinewy. But although we look ferocious, we're very peaceful.*

A: You seem to be very proud of your people.

J: *They are very family-oriented and very creative.*

A: What role do you play there with your people on Aurora?

J: *I'm their leader.*

A: Have you always been their leader?

J: *I sit in the halls of justice. The Great Hall is the largest hall that we have, which would be like your high court, your supreme court. But many people come to Aurora; they come to see me, for they need wisdom.*

A: What kind of wisdom do you give those that come to visit? What do you talk about with them?

J: *Energy.*

A: Can you tell me about this energy?

J: *How to hold energy, how to use energy, how to store energy, how to shape energy. If you think of clay and mould it into any shape, it's the same with energy, and energy creates form. So, it is how to create other planets.*

A: How do you do that?

J: *With thought, with lots of practice. I teach them, under the waterfall, in what you would say, a soccer ball or tennis ball size first, and get them to form them, and then they have to start adding to the form.*

They have to visualise different life forms, forms that are going to help that planet. So, I'm teaching them how to create miniature solar systems, but it takes immense self-governance, governance of self, and patience, temperance.

The ego has to be totally removed, for the entire planet of that solar system, all those planets within that miniature solar system, have to balance one against the other. You've got to work out the rotations, how they affect each other, what each need, you have to look at the oxygen levels, you have to look at the type of beings that are going to inhabit those areas.

Whether it is going to be a watery planet, what amphibians are going to be there, how they are going to live, do they need to eat what you term food? There's much to consider.

A: When one creates, manifests these worlds, is it just one being that does it, or do they have to do it together?

J: *Well, I've got to the point that I do it with my own power. That's my speciality, it is creation. As Jill in this incarnation is a very creative being with her interior design and with her writing, that is pulled through this fractal, but my abilities are supreme.*

Yet I do not have ego attached to it, but a love for teaching, for everything is balanced. For when I teach others balance, everybody, all the beings, gain from that.

For the more balance there is within, then the more balance there will be without — on the outside. For in nature, and in solar systems, it's all about balance, for if one goes off its axis, everything else… it is a ripple effect.

A: So, why is it that, at this time, Jill has been woken up, with the remembrance and the reminder of Aurora? What is important for her to understand now about it?

J: *This one always forgets who she is; she has much doubt. This fractal of Jill now is getting emotional, and even for this session, we wish to speak with you, Alba. She was once again doubting herself, and yet this is a good thing, for we wish to keep her humble, but we wanted to show her that she is a great teacher, and we wanted to bring her back to Aurora to show her what it was and is that she is teaching in Aurora, to many, many, many solar systems, because we wish for her to bring to humanity balance.*

Humanity has lost its balance. Its leaders are corrupt, they put themselves above their people when they should be working side by side. So, the balance needs to be restored, Alba. Everything is balance. For when one is top-heavy, things tip over, and you lose your balance, this is not what we wish to see.

A: So, how is it that Jill is balancing things out on this planet?

J: *Alba, through you and this one and this platform, you are reaching many, and you are reminding many what it is about balance. You recently had Covid arrive in your planet, not so?*

A: Yes, what was that all about?

J: *It was time to restore the balance within. So, how many mothers and fathers have had enough time with their children, Alba, for are they not busy bees? Working, working, working?*

They've lost the balance of what family is all about, and so Covid has arrived, and it is twofold. It is restoring the balance within families, reminding them of what is important, and it is going to reach a tipping point with your economy throughout this Earth plane, and it is what is termed a giant, for it is a sleeping giant, for the people of Earth.

They are the giant. The balance has gone too far the other way, and though the puppeteers are using Covid to manipulate the masses, the masses are now waking up, and they will once again find their balance.

A: What do you say to all those people who have lost their jobs, and are feeling so insecure at this time? Where is the balance there?

J: *In order to experience what it is to have an emotional experience, for this is an emotional plane, and many will have many emotions, losing loved ones, losing jobs, losing homes, but they came here, specifically, for this time period, to play their parts, and they are so embroiled in what we termed last session their meat suits that they forget that they are light beings, having an Earthly experience.*

But when many, many, many more start experiencing loss, whether it be financial, shelter, loved ones, this is a temporary experience. This is what will forge humanity to remember what it is to be humane, to support each other, for the great leveller is coming for all, and how will they respond, Alba?

A: Yeah, tell me about this leveller. What is happening?

J: *She's seeing it now. If one throws an incredibly large rock into a shallow pond, is there any part of that pond that will not be disturbed, or will all the water in the pond be disturbed?*

A: Everything.

J: *Everything, and those closest to the rock, will they experience the same turbulence, than those further away from the rock?*

A: No.

J: *It may be a different experience, but it will be an experience, nonetheless. There are many that are feeling an anticipation at this time, just as they did prior to Covid. We said to listen for the trumpet.*

A: To listen to the what?

J: *The trumpet.*

A: The trumpet.

J: *This one is trumpeting; she is speaking through us. We wish many to hear her words, for we wish to restore balance. We wish for humanity to look up the word sovereign, and regain their sovereign state. For did not one arrive here, as a light particle in love, for the All That Is? And what is one doing with one's photonic structure?*

There is a war going on, Alba, a war for the souls of humanity.

This one put on a song just before the session this morning. She wanted to play One Love *but Bob Marley decided to let her listen to another song, and it was termed* War. *It would be good for all to listen to the words of this song, but when we term the word war, how many, Alba, are at peace within themselves, or are they at war?*

For so many find so much imperfection within, and if there is a war going on internally, then the ripple effects will be external, and that is why there are what you term leaders who are not at peace within themselves, who are not holding balance, and then the people are experiencing the ripple effect. There is much that will soon be disclosed, Alba, then will people be steady, or will they react?

A: So, in your questions today we wanted to address the powerful nature of words and how we practice those words. Can you speak of that?

J: *We keep on speaking about words, and the power that words hold, and the words that people use for themselves and for another, or against another, and we wanted to use the word rumour.*

Rumour has it, so someone does not have a truth, someone does not hold the truth, however, humans want to be the centre of attention, even if it is for five seconds flat. But those five seconds can do incredible harm, for why would one spread a rumour? So, when we use the word rumour, how does it make one feel inside? Settled or unsettled? On Earth, you have what is called a dictionary, not so?

A: Yes, a dictionary.

J: *Filled with words, human words.*

A: Yes.

J: *How about playing with that dictionary, opening it up on any page, and testing the words or a word and feeling how that word feels inside? Do you not on the Earth plane have words that are called cuss words?*

A: Yes.

J: *Now, these words that are used to denigrate another shows you that the person using those words have lost their balance, for they no longer have control, for they have lost the art of communication and the art of communicating with themselves, for they have given their power away to another.*

Their battery, their generator, is depleting. For once they cuss and give that out to another, that load, those words that they are giving to another, will the other carry those words, or will they put the heavy metal shield up and bounce them right back? We see many humans with cuss words, they are still in kindergarten, those that give them and those that receive them. For those who have mastered themselves do not use these words, and those masters do not take those words on board.

Alba, there are very few who have mastered this, the ability to stand with both feet on the ground, well balanced and grounded and, as a result, there are many, many, problems that arise from the misuse of words.

A: Words certainly make a difference. I grew up in a family that did not use any cuss words. In fact, I was much older when I first heard one from anybody because my parents sheltered me from those words. My father always made sure that when I was with an adult that they spoke with me respectfully, and so now I am facing the same thing with my community in which — on my YouTube community — in which I expect the same respect of my clients, and it makes a big difference because I know that those words can hurt.

J: *Well, this one has, for the very first time, understood the words "lowers the tone." How many have heard the words lowers the tone, like you don't behave a certain way or you don't say something, because it just lowers the tone, it's just not good enough?*

But what do those words actually mean? What is a tone? A tone is a vibration, a tone is something that you get out of a musical instrument, and then what happens to that instrument if a tone is lowered? It can't play beautifully the way it is supposed to be heard.

It is like lowering the vibration, and we are all about lifting the vibration, and we would like to commend you, Alba, on being a regulator for higher vibrations, for when we look at corporations, and we look at the head of the corporation, they set the tone for the rest of the corporation. If you have what is termed a bully as a head of a department, then you will find that that works throughout that department or organisation, so it is all about holding the tone to a certain level.

Alba, as you regulate it, the others then will see what tone it is that you hold. If you are with humans who have great balance and mastery and respect for self, would you then lower the tone with them?

A: No.

J: *You don't, because they have set what is called a standard, and then it is like attracts like for those vibrations.*

For those who are of a lower vibration, who've been brought up around many cuss words, many lowering of vibrations, are struggling, they need help, they need love, they need balance, for there is disruption with them.

A: How do they do that? How do they get that balance when they are in a sea, when they are drowning in this low vibration?

J: *This is when I'd like to speak about the word emotion. This one did a hypnosis on a client over the weekend, and this particular human had a Master's degree, specifically in therapy regarding people's emotions, and yet although he holds a degree in the therapies, the emotion of people was not taught to the therapists at that level.*

He was so astute that he watched a programme called My 600-lb Life, *and yes, these people get gastric bands and operations, but that is not going to fix the problem of why they had the need to fill themselves from the outside in because they weren't dealing with the emotion.*

Your school systems teach children how to read, how to write, how to add up, teach them about areas of your Earth plane, but do they ever teach them about emotion, or their emotions Alba?

A: No, that's really not allowed.

J: *Alba, those children who are brought up by parents who know no better, who were brought up by parents who cussed, who took drugs to numb the pain, who used physical violence, these will be passed down through the generations and then you have a schooling system that does what you term the A B Cs, but they don't do the Ds and the Es, the domestic violence, and the emotions.*

So, this is a place where children can learn that it is okay to express an emotion in a healthy manner. I'm sad. I'm angry. I don't want to do that; this is the reason why I don't want to do that. But they hold it in, the anger builds, and so you have what is termed a bully, for they have been bullied in their home environment, and now they offset the hurt and the anger, and so they take it out on another, and they are never taught how to deal with that emotion.

(Jill stops to drink some water after coughing.) *It is apt that her throat is getting so affected.*

A: Why is that?

J: *Because this is the area that many need to clear. Because this, this is where the emotions sit and boil and it doesn't come out.*

A: Can we focus on that emotion that's there? What is that emotion that Jill has that hasn't come out? Feel the connection with the emotion. What is that emotion?

J: *Well, Jill, when she was young, was always taught to be quiet, to be seen and not to be heard, to be a good girl. So, if good girls can't be heard, mustn't be heard, what then does the good girl feel about herself?*

She then feels that she's not enough, and so the good girls get into relationships that are not suitable, but they don't speak up and they don't speak out, because that's not being a good girl. And many young boys are taught, do not cry, boys don't cry, be a man.

Your words are teaching humanity to hold everything in and down, and lower the tone, instead of allowing expression, and yet this builds over many years, and then you find human relationships, partners, lovers, friends who don't want to tell somebody something because they don't want to hurt their feelings, and there's tension, and there's resentment, and everything is governed by the emotion.

A: Let's identify that emotion that she is holding back. What is that emotion that Jill is holding down that is trying to escape? Hone in on it.

J: *She's literally coughing it up for all those that have been holding it in for so long. She has learnt very well how to speak up and how to speak out in a measured, balanced way, without manipulation.*

And that is key today — the word manipulation. Why would one need to use a manipulation in order to get one's way? A manipulation is used in many ways. So many men on this human plane go to what is termed a gym, to make themselves buff, and the girls walk around, showing off their assets, their external assets, for many of them have forgotten how to speak up and speak out, and they are expressing themselves through their bodies.

It's a way of saying look at me, notice me. We're not saying that you must not take pride in this meat suit, but we are saying that you can speak in a different manner.

There are many who are not being heard, Alba. It is time to speak up and to speak out and to speak their truth. How many countries, Alba, do you still have on your Earthly plane in the year 2020 where you deem one human to be above another, specifically of the female gender?

A: I don't think there's any.

J: *Where they've lost their power base, where men rule. Is this progress?*

A: That's a double-edged sword about truth, because if they have not been saying their truth for so long, those truths come out like daggers, with so much emotion.

J: *But that is because the emotion has not been taught as a subject, as a way of life, to philosophise about it, to hold it in. When one holds it in, how does one discuss it?*

How many families sit around the dinner table and discuss how each person's day has been, if the emotions have been met, how they are feeling, what is happening in their lives? Or do they sit in front of the blue box, disconnected from each other?

A: And texting.

J: *Yes, and these little children who run and fall and hurt their knees, and get brushed off and told you're a big boy, you're a big girl, come on everything is okay.*

So, when they get hurt as they grow older, they dust themselves off and say everything is okay and then they hold it in.

It is time for the discourse to begin and, Alba, because so many families are at discord with each other, they've lost the skills, or the education, of what it is to hold balance, for we would like to say today that a child has equal importance as an adult. Why would you talk down to a child just because they are smaller? Is that not abuse? Abuse comes in many forms, not just physical.

A: You have told us about the word GOSSIP — capital letters. Can you talk about that with us today?

J: *Gossip serves no one, for we would like to ask you, Alba, if the person you wish to gossip about was standing in front of you, would you still repeat the story?*

A: Not at all.

J: *Would you repeat the story?*

A: Not unless it was a funny one.

J: *If it was maligning to one, if it is what is termed bad-mouthing one, talking about somebody behind their back, another God spark, another light being. You're bringing the tone down about them, you're bringing the tone down about yourself. But what you are doing is you are pushing a load onto somebody else. For that person did not know that before and so you are placing a burden on another. Why would you do that to another, against another?*

For choices of how you treat others is how you treat yourself. And there are people that never gossip, and as a result, nobody ever gossips about them.

But how many of you, when somebody is gossiping to you about another, stand up and defend that one that is not there and say these are not my words, these are your words?

Because if you keep silent, are you then not compliant with that?

A: Yes, but it seems to me that all of the “news”, that we call news, in quotation marks is gossip.

J: *There is very little truth left in your media system. It is controlled by the few, over the many, but you have the power to turn off the blue box. Many have lost the art of self-entertainment, of entertaining oneself.*

So, one sits in front of the blue box and goes nowhere. We say treading water. If humans wish to regain their balance, then we suggest the monitoring of the blue box, for how many of those what you term “shows” are truly beneficial or uplifting?

A: Not too many of them, unless they’re about animals.

J: *The great show is within. All entertainment is within. We cannot reiterate this enough. If one does not go within, one goes without, and the energy we wish to speak of today, the generators, the powerhouses, the stations, these human stations, how are they living?*

Do they wish another to govern them, and how is that working for them? They are handing their power base over daily by watching the blue box, for when they watch the blue box, they are somnambulistic, they are not awake, they are not aware, they are switched off. Their machines are on snooze mode, for if they want change, they have to make a change, small changes within, changing of habits, more frequent communicating with each other, recognising the emotions.

How are they feeling?

How are they acting?

What makes them react?

Why are they reacting?

Why are they being triggered?

It is time for them to think on these, Alba.

A: Yes, thank you. I'd like to expand on something that Jill has been seeing in her mind — or hearing — is the word Shekinah. She was awoken with this word, Shekinah. Can you tell us why she's hearing that word?

J: *Because she is the light. She carries the light, and she holds the light for many. She is a beacon, she is a lighthouse, and Shekinah is a distributor, she is a sparkler, her photonic structure is structured in such a way that we would like to term the word chalice.*

She holds the eternal flame and, through the airwaves, your platform, we wish these lights, encoded words, to reach many. Alba, we are using her, to use her words in a very simplistic manner, for we wish all to understand.

She has the ability and the mind power to work on a very, very, high level, for did we not say that she will be dealing with governments in the future?

A: Yes, you did.

J: *For making changes to the system for humanity, she has that ability, she has that mind power. But what is the use of using hieroglyphics when one does not know how to decipher them?*

So, we are bringing the Shekinah through her to the people as a rock in a pond, for the ripples to spread, far and wide. For the torch beams, the pinpoints, the sunbeams, to penetrate into all the areas, for her words are light encoded, through the Shekinah and that is why you've had such a reaction to these sessions, for the people feel the resonance with them.

The Shekinah is in supplication with the ankh or the ankh (differing pronunciation), *the ancient Egyptian symbol, for did she not see, in the lobby of the pensione in Peru the AI, the being, the spaceship, the cog and the groove?*

Alba, you all needed to put your ankhs in each groove, your

Shekinah, for that group, (Jill and Alba's soul family) *holds much Shekinah, much light, for they are beacons of light.*

They are dispersed, like rays of light from the sun, solar flashes, in all areas of your Earth plane, holding the flame, the eternal flame. We chose this one as our mouthpiece for all the fractals that she is, for Uriel carries the light, for when she is in Aurora, she is the queen of balance, and that is what we wish for this Earth plane to see; the light of whom they are.

Alba, one such as you has the ankh. You have swallowed the ankh, it has travelled through you, it has connected you deeply with this one and others in the group, for we are showing her that ancient practice of feeding the pharaoh the ankhs. For when one has the Shekinah, the light aligned, then one can be a way-shower.

We do not all need to be leaders, we wish people to be a way-shower, and if you on your Earth plane have cities with street after street, do they not have lights showing the way? And so, they are a way-shower, for there is no danger in the light. Alba, we wish for all to be filled with the ankh, the eternal flame, and the Shekinah.

A: Just for those who are listening who don't know what an ankh is. Is this a physical thing or is it a symbolic thing?

J: *It is energetic. Ooh, and this one is feeling the most peculiar sensation. Something's happening all through her now* (Jill points towards the left side of her face) *and the ankh and the symbol, the energy put around that symbol, stimulates the third eye and opens it to let in the direct line.*

It is aligning with all the fractals that the cell is, in the total body of the All That Is. It is a key, Alba, the ankh is a key to unlock life that has been trapped, to get it free-flowing.

But we want to come back to the blue box. How does one get back to the stillness, and the connection, and the unlocking of the light for all?

For all are coded with light, for all are light bodies, but because they forget, they get so embroiled in what you term nonsense that they're not living fully. They are allowing others to govern them in a nonsensical way, for they do not have way-showers who are running these countries on this Earth plane.

They have leaders who put themselves above, instead of working side by side with their people.

Who are their people but born, just like they are? All are equal. The way-showers are the ones that spread the light for others to see. It is time for keys to be unlocked, and for those who are watching today, we wish for them to find a quiet spot, close their eyes.

Alba, we would like them to go to your website. On your website, you have a meditation. During that meditation, they will have a connection with themselves, and they will start turning the key. You, Alba, are a way-shower. (www.albaweinman.com)

A: I guess I signed up for this, huh?

J: *You certainly did. A wild ride!*

A: Sure is. So, when we started this today, we were on the planet Aurora with this being that was the queen. How is that influencing that Jill has here as a way-shower?

J: *Jill meets with her, in Aurora, with others, teaching balance, and currently she is working on a new solar system, for when the great leveller arrives on Earth, many will be going to their way-stations, and then they will need to gain their balance and their perspective.*

Alba, this one has just remembered something. Her father, as you know, has recently passed away, and you have one called Shera, who does the work that you and that this one does.

A: In Egypt, yes.

J: *Yes, in Egypt, in her home base, and her father came through Shera with a message for her. This one and Shera found out that her father is learning from this one.*

Shera and this one thought that once you pass over through your way-station that you only learn on the other side, that they don't then learn from us here, from the beings on Earth.

She then connected with her father last week, and had a chat with him, and asked him what he was up to, he said that he was in the waiting room. She had never heard this terminology about a waiting room. He passed away from this Earth plane through the way-station to the council of the wise, and at the moment he's attending classes, learning about many different things.

Then he is in his waiting room to see where he will go next, where his next adventure will be, where his expansion will be, what he wishes to develop or experience. So, those on Earth who will no longer be here after the great leveller, we would like to thank them for the immense work that they are doing, through ascension, with Gaia, with this Earth plane, for they have come through their star-seeded lineage to help Gaia to get back with her brothers and sisters, her grandparents, for she is a very young planet, and she needs to ascend.

It is time for her graduation, and many came here for the change in many different parts.

So please, Earthlings, with their emotions, feel the emotions, but celebrate the joy, for those who will what you term pass away will not be gone. For is this one not communicating with her father? He has not gone; he has changed form, vibration.

He is having a new dance. So, those that will leave for the energy that is coming, for some, it will be too much for them because they have not done the work, for they have been slumbering.

They have been on snooze mode in front of the blue box. They have disconnected from this life. They are living on this Earth, this beautiful, beautiful Earth plane, and they are not connecting with the Earth. They are not grounded; they are just floating.

This one on Aurora is at the moment very busy creating a very beautiful new solar system, with planets that will rest and rejuvenate these fractals of souls. When they have rested, it will be like a holiday, a vacation. They have much to look forward to. We wish for all the relatives who are left behind to comfort them and to know that they are going to a place of peace and tranquillity, in order to regain their balance and align them with the All That Is.

A: For those who have not been following this, and hear about this great levelling, can you explain that briefly? What that is? Because it sounds catastrophic.

J: *How does one deal with catastrophe?*

One deals with catastrophe as to how one is. How one knows oneself, and that is why we repeatedly say, who are you, what do you live for, who do you live for? You've all come for ascension, you have come for Gaia, and you have come for the galaxies and the multiverse.

Who are you?

You are a spark of light.

You are a light being.

You are a light traveller, travelling through space, time.

There is no beginning, there is no end.

Yet you think you are nothing but a human form, and when you are nothing but a human form then there is catastrophe, and there is great fear. That is why we want people to know who they are, to remove the fear.

A: Very good, thank you. Would you like to explain why you brought up birthdays and *Christmas?*

J: *Yes. What is a birthday? It is the day you arrived on this domain. Each year of that birth is a commemoration, a remembrance, a thanksgiving because you made a decision to be here, and yet what do humans do? A lot of them go out, they imbibe, they become senseless; they do not connect with themselves.*

They buy each other gifts, many with money that they do not have, in order to say happy birthday. Alba, imagine on a birthday, everybody writes a poem, or a letter to the person, telling the person what they feel about the person, why they are joyful to have that person in their life. That is a true present, for it is words, and words, as we know, hold great power. Fresh flowers, take them for a walk, lean against a tree, have a picnic, connect with nature.

How many of you have received birthday presents that you do not know what to do with, that you re-gift, put somewhere on the shelf, and think to yourself, wow, if that person arrives, where did I put that gift, because it doesn't resonate with me?

Humans have to rethink what a birthday really means. We just wanted to give a new way of looking at a birthday, we want to take away the consumer side of birthdays and honour the being.

A: Good. What about Christmas? Same thing?

J: *Now, Christmas. We mentioned, and this one spoke to you briefly about it before we started this discourse today. There are many who are not what you term Christians, so it could be Hanukkah, it could be Eid, it could be Thanksgiving, it could be any specific day, even Halloween. Any specific day, where a lot of attention is given.*

So, Christmas Day is on the 25 December, but it is a day like any other day. It could be 13 July or 5 January, but everybody knows Christmas, everybody puts immense energy towards Christmas, and that is what makes it special.

There is a special effort, and whatever you put your energy

towards, expands and grows.

What we want to say is, we're using Christmas Day as an example of energy, where you expend your energy. So many of you may never get to Christmas, may take your last breath before Christmas, so what about this given day, this hour, this minute, this moment, giving yourself the energy of Christmas every day. Bring the energy, make the effort to make it special, for it is nothing other than the output that creates that moment.

A: Wonderful. It sounds like a great plan. It's up to us to do it.

J: *Yes. You have many that suffer during Christmas, those who are homeless, those who are separated, those who have discord in families. There are many suicides over this time period, for many feel the aloneness, for the energy is out of proportion, and what has become a celebration which should be about putting time away or aside for family, has become a time for consumerism.*

What happens to all the wrappings? What happens to all the ribbons? What happens to all the cards? What about gifting your time to those less fortunate than you at Christmas? That may be a better proposition than consumerism.

A: I guess the way-showers need to step it up.

J: *Yes. Once again, it's about balance.*

A: Is there anything else that you want to touch on today?

J: *One is coughing again because one wants to remind many about speaking out.*

What is one holding in that one is too afraid to speak out about at this time?

There's much that will create unsettlement ahead, but please do look at the sun, and remember the light. Daily, look at the sun and know that you have the power, that brightness, within. Do not allow another to dim your light, to turn down your wattage, for when one does this to another, it is nothing but a reflection of what is going on in that particular human.

Please to know that the humans that denigrate others are the ones that are not full inside. They actually need comforting, they need to be heard, they need to be held, the violent ones, the cussing ones. They hold great hurt for they have not been taught about the emotion.

This one would like to speak about Mr Wright, the one who has the Master's degree and mastered emotion. For if there are organisations listening today, education specifically, kindergartens, schools, universities and corporations, this one can put them in touch with Mr Wright.

He will feel the pulse of the corporation, the institution and will be able to help them with the emotions.

It will be like giving them a warrant of fitness, there are many that need a warrant of fitness with their emotions at this time.

A: Very good, thank you so much. What are we calling this session today?

J: *Balance.*

A: Beautiful. Is there anything you would like to tell others at this time?

J: *Yes. Many who have listened to this may be holding a lowered tone through fear, for they know not who they are.*

Please to remember who you are. You are part of All That Is; there's no separation. Should you leave this Earth plane, or your family members leave this Earth plane, please do not buy into the dogma of certain institutions and ancient stories that have told you about terrible places where loved ones may go, for we are one, we work together for the light and in the light.

Let there be light with the new you.

So be it.

A: Wonderful, thank you so much. Who are we speaking with

today?

J: *James, Jesus's brother.*

A: Thank you, James, for this message today, and we look forward to hearing from the team soon. Thank you so much.

CHAPTER SEVEN (Session 416)

I AM FREEDOM

In this hypnosis session Jill encounters Jesus's disciple, Simon, who is stricken with grief and fear over the judgment and crucifixion of his Master. The session focuses on judgment, equality, preparation for the incoming energetic wave of the ascension, and the help and awareness needed for the broken boys and girls.

A: Where are you?

J: *I can feel that there are beings around me, but it's almost like they're in the shadows.*

A: So, I'd like you to go ahead and begin to open up those other senses where you can hear them. Begin to hear the flow once again. What are they discussing today?

J: *I hear the word judgement. They're talking about judgement.*

A: They're talking about judgement. How many of these shadows do you see?

J: *Twelve. They are the disciples.*

A: They are the disciples. Who's coming forth?

J: *Simon.*

A: Why has Simon stepped forward today?

J: *For Jesus, for the judgement that Jesus has received.*

A: You can connect with their hearts and souls and can feel it.

J: *We are bereft* (Jill starts crying). *Such judgement for one that is so pure of heart.*

A: What has caused so much judgement for one man?

J: *He is showing the people that there's another way, and the powers that be don't want the people to be free, and so they had Him removed.*

A: How did that affect everyone who is learning from Him and following Him?

J: *We are disoriented, we are bereft, and we are scared, for if they did that to Him, we are next in line. So, we have to scatter, we have to get our belongings, we have to find our women and our children, and we have to put them into hiding, for some of the children are too young to travel with us, and they are our beloveds as well, and so we are separated once again.*

But we are more determined than ever to continue this work, for we see now what a threat freedom is to the powers that be, for if He was not speaking the truth, He would still be with us.

A: Simon, can you talk to me about freedom? What is freedom? What are they afraid of?

J: *They don't want you to know who you are. They want ownership because they want to tax you. For taxation is all that's important to them, but they do not realise that if the people are free to be who they are, taxations will come in a different manner.*

Taxations will be given with love, for it will be for their fellow man and for their families, to provide nourishment, housing, education, clean water, teaching. There won't be a yoke around them, for are they not a particle in the pulse of All That Is?

A: Yes.

J: *So, why would one want to contain a cell in the All That Is, and not let it roam free?*

A: Is that what Jesus was teaching? (Jill is nodding)

J: *Our master, and He did not like to be called that, for He was not one about control or power, but He was the supreme way-shower. Wherever He went, the light fell in abundance, for He had so much love within Him, and as a result, it came out of Him and showered like the rain on all.*

There was not one that He did not love: beggars, thieves, royalty, prostitutes, businessmen, housewives, all were equal.

A: I'm sure that the master... (Jill interrupts her.)

J: *He wanted to show them.*

A: What did He want to show?

J: *Sorry, Alba?*

A: What did He want to show?

J: ***He wanted to show them that they are God.***

When they said, "in my image" we arrived in His image, in this current 3D form, but He or It, or the Power, or the Source, or the Strawberry Jam, he has many forms, we have many forms.

Our current form is as a 3D Earthling, but this is not who you are.

This is the coat that you wear, and so we come back to judgement. This one today has put on a pearl necklace, she has put on pearl earrings, she looks different to the other sessions. She even put waves in her straight hair.

We did this because we wanted to speak about judgement. Today she is wearing something called a jersey, a jumper, or a cardigan. It is made out of soft cashmere. These are things, these pearls, these waves, this cashmere, does not define who this being is.

It is exterior. This being could have on a raggedy dress, no waves, no cashmere, no pearls, and her essence would remain the same. However, Earthlings have been taught to judge one another, and why? Why does one judge another? For our master was judged, and those that you judge today, not only are you crucifying them, but you are crucifying yourselves, for did it not say judge not, lest ye be judged?

A: Yes.

J: *So, when you judge one that has what you deem to be better than what you are, from the trappings, then you feel less than, and you put them on an elevated status. But this is not who they are. They are not better than you, or less than you, because of their trappings.*

Those that judge somebody else for their trappings are entrapped themselves, and those that have the trappings, and think they are better than another, they are entrapped as well.

So, today, we want people, as we said in our last session, to look in the mirror, and if there's going to be any judgement, please, let us not look at the exterior, let us start pulling everything that's

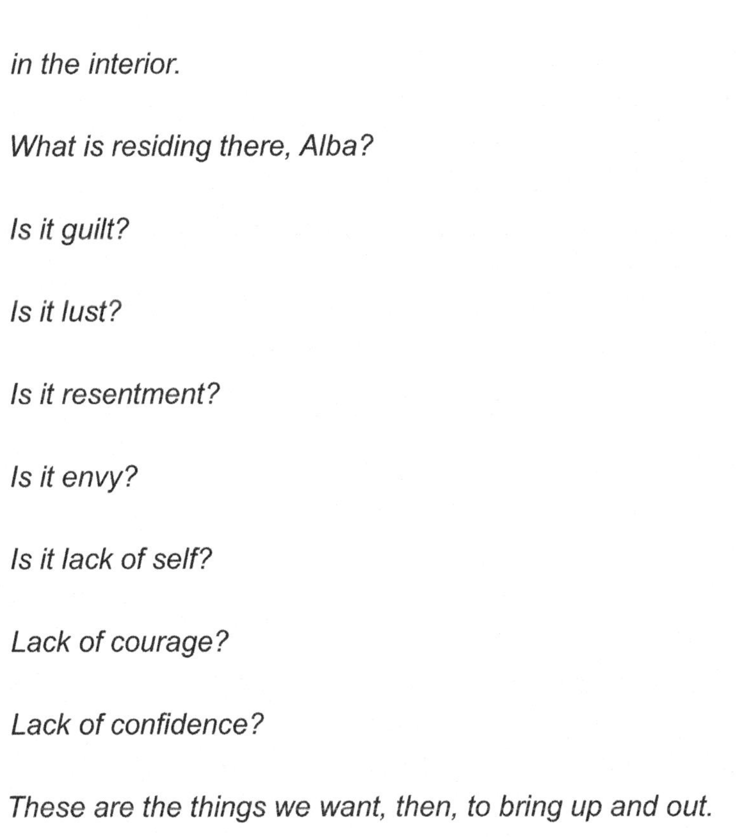

in the interior.

What is residing there, Alba?

Is it guilt?

Is it lust?

Is it resentment?

Is it envy?

Is it lack of self?

Lack of courage?

Lack of confidence?

These are the things we want, then, to bring up and out.

For we are saying the day of judgement is nearing. There is a quickening in the multiverses. The energy is getting closer and closer. And that is why we say know thyself.

This is the time for cleaning, this is a time for cleansing, this is a time for consciousness. This is a time for the great awakening. One cannot reach ascension if one has not woken up.

So, our master came to teach us all about truth, and the truth is who you are. No one controls you. You came here on this Earth plane to partake on a mission, as a light being, as a spark of God. You are boundless, and you are everywhere, and as she puts her hand on her chest, she is feeling her vibration, her frequency.

Alba, we wish you to put your hand on your chest.

A: Yes.

J: *Is your hand on your chest?*

A: Yes, it is.

J: *Alba, we now wish for all those who are listening (and reading this book) to now press firmly their hand on their chest, and we wish them to say: "I am." Repeat after me, Alba — "I am."*

A: I am.

J: *Louder.*

A: I am.

J: *One more time, Alba.*

A: I am.

J: *What did you feel?*

A: It is a very strong vibration.

J: *Now, Alba, we wish everybody to say:*

I am a spark of light.
I am a light being.
I come from the All That Is.
There is no end.
I am boundless.
I have nothing to fear because I am.

A: That's quite a mouthful.

J: *They need to write this down; they need to press what you term pause on this transmission, and they need to lie down like this one, and they need to proclaim who they are this given day, for they are the power and the glory.*

Let there be no misunderstanding on this given day of whom they are. It is time for them to claim their sovereignty, for the All I Am wishes to expand.

A: Now that we've declared that, can you tell me more about this day of judgement, and why must we declare this?

J: *Alba, do you not work with many beings under hypnosis?*

A: Yes.

J: *Do you not have those souls who have fragmented, who need to go back to the All That Is? Do you not allow them to heal themselves into wholeness before they return to the light?*

A: Yes.

J: *Right, this procedure is so humanity carries a lighter load. When a lighter load is carried, when they say the I am, their resonance goes up. Their resonance lightens, their frequency goes onto a different channel.*

When it is low, it is like a valley peak, and they are at the bottom of the peak, and having to climb up. When it is higher, it is much shorter and faster, and so the transmission is a higher frequency. When it is a higher frequency, we, their guides, can transmit a lot smoother and a lot faster with them.

We wish them to lose the baggage that they carry before they get onto the supersonic highway, for as the new energy arises, there will be much friction on Earth.

There will be dissatisfaction, there will be rumblings, and as we said before, many will what you term pass away. But they will know who they are. They would have accomplished their mission. Do you not have on all your foodstuff, a "best by date", or a "used by date"?

A: Yes, expiration date.

J: *An expire-ation date. No more* (Jill breaths out) *no more breath. It will have expired. However, they will be done when they have done what they have come to do. Some have short lives, some have longer lives; one is not better than the other. But how many humans are living fully, with the breath that they have at the moment?*

They are so busy judging one another, feeling less than, or superior to another, that they've forgotten the brotherhood, what it is to be loved and to enjoy each other's company, for they are fixated with the blue box, with the latest fashion, and trying to keep up with the Joneses.

It is so much nonsense, so much time wasted when they could be connecting internally with us; and with the All That Is. For all will sit in front of the wise council. The wise council will not be judging them, for they are wise, for all these beings on Earth will be judging themselves.

How did they do? Could they have done better? Did they have the opportunity to wake up? Did they have the opportunity to assist not only themselves but another? For, Alba, the greatest service that one can give oneself is to assist another, for there are great lessons to be learnt when giving of oneself. For one also needs to receive help from another.

It is very easy to give to another, but it is very hard to receive from another.

A: Yes.

J: *One has to realise one has value and there are so few humans who realise their value, but we would like to say, every single human incarnation on this Earth plane now have incredible value, are part of this beautiful planet, and are part of ascension. Many are lying low. Many, after hearing this transmission, will rise and meet the challenge.*

A: It is challenging at this time. In our own country here in the United States, they are doing everything they can to separate us, by gender, by colour, by sexual preferences, by money, by everything.

They're keeping us physically apart; they're masking us so we can't see each other. Why so many difficulties at this time, right before judgement day?

J: *Because, when somebody makes gold bullion, it's put under incredible pressure. Only then does the purity come out, and this is all part of what is termed 'the rising.'*

This one is now being shown a painting that she did, a sketch, many years ago, almost 20 years ago, and we gave her a vision of a king on a throne, hewn out of rock, and that king was called Christ.

Behind the throne was the sun rising, and there were people coming out of the sun. It looked as if they were coming out of the sun.

Women, children, men, walking and walking and walking, all together, coming to discover a new land and a new Earth, and it was as if they were the sun, for they were light beings, they were beings of light.

Not heavy beings, not dragging around 30kg, but it was a new way and a golden era. But how does one get the golden era without removing the dross?

This current period in your Earth plane has much corruption, has much darkness, and the agitation will increase as the energy comes closer. This energy that is coming closer is a present to the human race as it is lifting the tempo. It is lifting the vibrations. It is lifting the people to rise above. And when we say rise above, we say rise above those that will have you shackled and yoked for the taxations, for the corruption and the power of holding mankind down.

When this energy arrives, as the tempo lifts, as the economies collapse, as work disappears, as the systems start to crumble, many will think this is catastrophic.

But they are the light warriors that have come here for ascension. They are strong, this is but temporary.

This agitation has to occur in order for the old ways to fall away for this is not how humanity is supposed to live. This is not thriving, this is surviving.

Humanity got a small taste during lock-up. Covid, what it was to reunite with their loved ones without the stress of having to go to work.

Now, that feeling, Alba, that they had, many had not had this feeling for a long time. Many had not slept in, rested their bodies for a very, very long time. For they were on the treadmill, the constant treadmill of humanity to buy things they don't need, to keep up with the Joneses, to feel that they fit in and that they belong. And that they have value.

They have been marketed by the puppeteers through that blue box to always feel less than, to always feel that they have to have the bigger house, the better clothes, the bigger car to have value, and so they are enslaved.

They have been separated by being told they're superior because they are a different colour to another but let me tell you that our Father in heaven, the All That Is, made every living being.

No one colour, nationality, or culture is superior or inferior to another.

For when you bake a delicious cake and you leave out all the beautiful bits, you're not going to have the flavour. In the golden era which will be visited upon the Earth plane, many will, for the first time, see what it is to be human.

We know this is a very, very, long answer to your question, but this is very, very important because we wish humanity to be gentle with themselves, we wish them to forgive themselves, for what they have been taught, or termed is a sin, most of these so-called sins are nothing other than lessons to be navigated to know who you are.

Be truthful with yourselves, be truthful with your loved ones, give yourself something that you term "slack", give yourselves a little slack. But be true to yourselves, for when you stand before yourself and the wise ones, you want to be as crystal as possible, and the more crystal that you are now, day by day, when the great leveller comes, and the energy gets closer, you will be stronger.

You will be firm in your resolve, and you will not allow yourself to be coerced by those in government and governance who wish you harm.

As we said before, we do not wish for a revolution externally, with violence. We want peaceful sittings, we want people side by side, for you are all a link on the chain, and this one has been shown an image of an enormous metal hammer, from the power and the corruption, and they are wanting, like a sledgehammer, to break all the chains of brotherhood, for when you unite and remember who you are in your sovereignty, there is no one government that can control you, for you are your own control.

Let all be free, and we end this particular question with the hand on the chest and say, "I AM."

A: I am.

J: *Thank you, Alba.*

A: Thank you for that. I have so many questions about this wave of energy coming. People have talked about an event that's coming. They've shown it in their mind as being physical, as a light. They've shown it as being other things. When will we be able to know that we are in this wonderful energy?

J: *Alba, it is getting closer. Many are feeling very fatigued. This is one of the signs. We wish humanity to drink lots of water, more so than usual, for your cell structures need water, for they plump up with water, and they will hear our transmissions and our guidance, this is a time to be guided.*

This energy that arrives will be of a frequency that you have not assimilated into your human structures before, and that is why we need water and rest. Because it is of such a high frequency, it will affect weather, it will affect tectonics, the plate structures holding the continents in place.

There will be many upheavals physically and internally. We wish humans to stop stuffing themselves with foodstuffs at this time because when they eat to excess, or when they put dross inside this fine system, they are weighing themselves down.

If there is a turbulence and you have a feather, the feather will float above, but if you were a rock, the rock would be heavy. It would fall, and it would have a lot of turbulence. That is why we want people to stop judgement, to know who they are, to be the finest specimen that they could be.

When humans arrive on this Earth plane and they are what is termed babies, if you put a toddler on a beach, would that toddler point to different people on the beach and say, "Oh, I can't play with you; you don't have the latest swimsuit on?"

A: No.

J: *"I can't play with you because you're the wrong colour. I can't play with you because you're not my religion." A toddler would not say that. So, why would a bigger toddler say that?*

These people call themselves adults, but they are not adult.

We want adults to have a toddler mindset, loving everybody, playing with everybody, accepting everybody.

When did the toddler learn to judge? When did the toddler learn to think they were separate from their brother?

The All That Is did not produce human form to be separate, but rather to enhance one another through their different abilities, their different gifts, their different recipes, their different cultures.

You should be sharing and celebrating with joy the differences, rather than fighting each other and separating.

Do not let those in governance divide you from another.

A: Thank you very much. You had written the word equality for us. Is that what you're speaking of?

J: *This is what we are speaking of; equality. We would like human beings, each one that is listening to this transmission now, to make what you term posters with the word EQUALITY.*

Put them on their car windows, put them in their house windows, wear them on their chests, make a banner, we want equality for all.

We spoke about judgement and now we speak about equality. Do you think that somebody in the poorest part of your country, if he stands in front of a judge, what you call a judge, in a house of court, will he get the same judgement as one of those humans who come from what you term a privileged background?

A: No, not at all.

J: *Why, Alba?*

A: That's the way of the courts. That's the way of the people; they judge.

J: *But is this justice?*

A: No, it is not.

J: *Is that called justice for all?*

A: No.

J: *So, Alba, what does your constitution say?*

A: Freedom and justice for all.

J: *So, Alba, where are the banners? Why do we have to have a movement called Black Lives Matter? Life matters. In any colour. In any shape or form.*

All lives matter.
Justice for all.
Equality for all.
Judgement for none.

A: It's going to be a different world.

J: *Alba, it's up to the people. We said in our last session the giant is sleeping; the giant are the people.*

Why do the people allow their sovereign rights to be taken away? We do not wish for them to blame the governments, for once again, that is lack of responsibility of self, for is not self-responsible for self?

A: Yes.

J: *If one has not stood up and said, "enough is enough" how can one then blame another? One has a voice box, does one not?*

A: Yes.

J: *It's time for the pulse, it is time for the finger, the third finger once again, to rest in the base of one's throat, and as one said before, "I am" on the chest, we wish them to put their finger deeply in the crevice of their throat — that's where their voice box is — and say,*

"I am sovereign.

I control myself.
I am part, of the All That Is.
No one separates me.
I separate myself from another.
It is time to claim back my freedom.
So be it."

A: Thank you. I want to focus now on how we become so judgmental and so broken. You have spoken about domestic violence and the broken boy. How do we stop the wheel of violence?

J: *Alba, there is a very strong movement that we see taking place on your Earth plane. You know, it started off with the "Me Too" movement, then it moved to "Black Lives Matter" and now we see "Save the Children."*

A: Yes.

J: *Humans get very emotional when it's their children, but people listening to this transmission are what are termed adults. But how do you become an adult, unless you too were a child once? Isn't that how it goes; baby, child, teenager, adult?*

A: That's right.

J: *So, we speak of the broken boys and the broken girls who are now adults and although they are adult in size, there's a broken boy and a broken girl inside these adult beings.*

(Jill starts crying.) *This one is crying for them, for she feels their pain, and as they were broken little boys and little girls, they grew up with frustration and anger and sorrow.*

For they were not cared for when they were little and now they are broken big boys and broken big girls, and so they hurt the others through domestic violence.

They know not how to cope with the hurt and the pain, for they lack communication and value of self, for they know not who they are, and their parents did not know who they were, for the controllers and the puppeteers have controlled for centuries.

So, the violence, the domestic abuse, continues. So, yes, it is so important to save the children, but who are going to save the broken big boys and the broken big girls?

We would like a community to begin, just like "Me Too", "Black Lives Matter", "Save the Children." We now want something to start, and it's "Save the Big Broken Boys and Girls." Let them step forward, let them form a community, let them not play victim, let them get in touch with Angela and Jason Wright.

(A banner is displayed on the screen showing The Feelings Counsel, a Facebook group where people could get in touch with them.)

Let them be taught the emotional skills. Let us break the old ways, the broken ways, and let us heal these broken boys and girls.

We said in our last session that much will be disclosed, as these broken big boys and broken big girls come up and speak out, and join forces, and have each other.

They will be able to expose much darkness, but those perpetrators have been broken themselves, so where does one start, and where does one stop?

How much love does one hold?
How much judgement does one hold?
Does one hold more anger in oneself than forgiveness and love?

At some stage, everything has to come up and out. It is a tribunal for human justice and forgiveness.

A: So, for those that are listening right now that are broken, what would you like to tell them?

J: *They can contact Jill, she is known as the connector, for she connects many. She knows the avenues and the people that can be put together, for today she connected many with their hearts, for now they are waking up.*

Alba, your platform is one of light, it is light-infused. Your team and our team are working in unity to raise the vibrations of each human that hears these words. For today, this transmission will be one of the most powerful yet, for each human who listens to this will be touched, and they will share this transmission with many, for there are many that are broken, but it is a time of healing and purity and fresh beginnings.

A: Wonderful. You spoke about timing and alignment on your list. Is that something we've already discussed?

J: *We wish to speak about timing, and we wish to speak about alignment.*

A: Thank you.

J: *And what is timing, and what is alignment? But they work together. This one now has spoken of Angela, who resides in the country called Australia, and Jason Wright, who lives in your country, America. She spoke to you this morning of a man called Steve Dix, who comes from this one's homeland in South Africa, but has moved to Australia. We, this one's team, have been working on a timeline to put them together with another from Australia, who worked with the Children's Commission Monique. They will be working with the broken ones, with the big broken ones and the little broken ones.*

This one recently did a reading for a lady in New Zealand who had been sexually molested by a step-brother. When she did the reading, the guides came through and used a term "she took one for the team", and it meant the team for humanity, for she has immense strength.

She is a detective and we put her into that job because she will be able to set up a program for the children to speak out whenever they've been told, "Sshhhhh, this is a secret, don't tell anyone."

She will be working with Jason, Angela, Stephen, and the one from the Child Commissioner. All these only came together in the last two months, for none of them were aligned beforehand; they were all in their own journeys, and we had to assimilate many different beings over many different continents to work together at the same time.

But humanity always wants to have it now, but the time has to be aligned, so those that are listening, that want to make a difference, please know that just by listening to our words today, through this one, our messenger, our ambassador from the Intergalactic Federation of Light that sits with Jesus.

Please know his essence is coming through this one today. His great love for you all and the energy that is coming for the rising for you all, is the energy of the Christ, the love, and the light.

Will you all rise to the occasion?

A: Thank you. Something else we wanted to discuss was reading people's energy from emails, and Facebook, and things like that. There was a thing that you put there, you called it a befriendment request. Would you like to talk about our social media?

J: *The reason we put this out there… this one has a big heart.*

She doesn't want to reject anyone, but she gives and she gives and she gives, and we don't wish for this one to be exhausted by the giving so that she can't be our mouthpiece.

So, we would like to put a request to all that listen or read these words. By all means, connect with her — she has much to offer. She can connect you with many groups, but she will be setting up a separate Facebook page for all of you, and then she'll have a separate one for her close friends and her family.

There have been a few that have been befriending her, and she sees that they have mutual friends, but when she speaks to the mutual friend to find out about the one that is befriending her, that mutual friend does not know that person, and yet they're befriending them.

So, what actually is this all about, Alba? We want people to read the energy of another, for not all are aligned. So, this one is now reading the energy of friendships through what's termed Facebook, and she's reading the energy that comes in via emails, although we wish this one to no longer do readings, for it is stressing her too much. She needs to spend and focus her energy now on The Discourse.

She needs to type up the book and then get the book into audio form.

That is where we wish for her energy to be expelled. She is fully booked until the end of September. We will allow her to take new clients until the end of October, but we are seeing that she is beginning to stress for she wishes to please so many, and yet she has not been out for a walk and connected with nature, for she is giving to others and not to self, yet she teaches others to give to self before they give to another.

That is why we wish to make this broadcast about befriendment; she does not wish to upset or reject any.

A: Thank you. I would think that's the same for everyone else, that they should also be reading and connecting with those who vibrate the same as them.

J: *Correct.*

A: OK, very good.

J: *On their colour wave, Alba.*

A: What is it?

J: *On their colour wave.*

A: On their colour waves, that's right. Very good. So, is there anything else you would like to express today?

J: *Alba, this one doubts herself, over and over. This was our eighth session; this was a dedication to Simon the disciple.*

A: Yes.

J: *She is our mouthpiece; we will not let her down. She never wants to disappoint, as she has great love for humanity, she feels their pain, she feels their anxiety. But yesterday we would like to thank you for the gift you gave her, for our master stepped forward, and connected with her in her heart.*

The vibrations the humans felt today through this one was the Christ light from our Father.

A: Beautiful, thank you.

J: *Alba, we would like to thank you so much for the beautiful work that you honour us with.*

A: Thank you.

J: *Thank you, Alba.*

A: Thank you. Who are we speaking with today? Are we speaking with Simon, or Urka, or someone else?

J: *Today, you are speaking through the fractal of Jesus and Simon combined, for they are a brotherhood.*

A: Wonderful, thank you so much. What do we call this session today? Is it judgement?

J: *Freedom, I am.*

A: Freedom, I am, is that right?

J: *Correct.*

A: Thank you so much. Thank you for the transmission.

J: *Sorry Alba, correction. We would like to transverse that.*

A: I am freedom?

J: ***I AM FREEDOM***

A: That sounds much better. Thank you so much for this, and I'd like to thank all of the guides assisting with this, with Jill, with me, and all of those who are listening. Thank you for joining us here today, with your collective love and vibration. Thank you for that. Are we complete?

J: *We are complete.*

A: Thank you so much.

CHAPTER EIGHT (Session 419)

DOUBT

In this hypnosis session we continue our discourse as Jill channels her guides. When she encounters Jesus, we talk about doubts. The session focuses on the importance of self-acceptance and self-care. We are asked to declutter our lives and minds. We also discuss Gaia's ascension and the great leveller.

J: *Jesus.*

A: Jesus? where is he?

J: *He's standing in front of me.*

A: He's standing in front of you, what does he tell you?

J:*To be kinder to myself.*

A: What has happened to Jill that she has not been kind to herself?

J:*She's taken on a responsibility of the mission, and she has embraced it so fully that she has forgotten to put herself first.*

A: How is that affecting Jill?

J: *She's not sleeping, she's not grounding herself. The responsibility of the mission weighs heavily. She is still doubting herself.*

A: Why so much doubt, not only from Jill but from those who listen to these sessions? Why is there so much doubting?

J: *Because we brought her here, and her main job is to teach people who they are, that they are light beings, and although she has transmitted this message over and over, and she has had so many experiences with us, she still looks in the mirror and she sees a small Jill.*

She does not wish for arrogance for she never sees herself as one that is better, or higher than another, so this is weighing heavily on our sister's shoulders.

A: How are those in the divine realm helping her?

J: *We have Simon Peter here; we have James and they are working with her.*

A: But she still doubts?

J: *Yes, her earthly incarnation is as a Jill, so she sees her faults and she still cannot understand why they would choose her, for she does not feel worthy of this mission.*

Although her heart is full, and she is a supreme teacher, her passion is for learning, and for spreading her knowledge.

A: So why is she doubting? Why did she choose to be so small in this body?

J: *To remind everybody that positions in life don't make you who you are, but it is the essence that comes from the heart, what radiates out of your being that is what designates your greatness.*

A: So, can you give her a visual of this essence that she puts out? Can you show her?

J: *She sees it now. She is a pillar of light. We radiate through this one, sending her photonic structure across the vibrations of the transmission to reach many.*

A: What happens when they receive this message? How does that affect them?

J: *She is being shown the image of a doll that she had as a little girl. When you wind it up at the back it started to move. So, it is like an old-fashioned metal key, and it is associated with the symbol of the ankh.*

For those two are connected as a key, to open up and to unlock the vibrations that all hold within is light because they are made of the photon, so the light particle needs a gentle reminder, an energy booster, for did we not say, many sessions ago, that she is a generator, an energy generator?

So she will be boosting those photons, she will kick them into a new rhythm. It is similar to when one has a heart attack and they put the machine on to kick them back into place. It's just an extra jolt.

A: Okay, now, I've been receiving these extra jolts from Jill for a while, and it seems it's affected my photons in a very strange way. What can we expect to see in the future with our bodies as we receive these messages, and as our bodies begin to adjust?

J: *She was given an example two nights ago about the saying, "Are you worth your weight in gold?" and she thought about this, and the more she thought about it, the more she didn't want to discuss this with the audience, for she felt it was judgemental, but we showed her those who have a condition called bulimia, then we showed her those humans who have a condition called obesity.*

Both of those conditions are governed by the photonic structure and the vibrations with the thought processes of trauma. Traumatic experiences, past experiences of the trauma, held in those bodies.

So, one has a weight, and the other one is a light weight, and what of the balance? The balancing of the emotions?

So, those two photonic structures need adjustments and old programs that need to be removed.

Then this one thought about her weight and what it was that she was worth, for was she worth her weight in gold? And when we mean gold, we mean the treasure inside. This one has been putting on weight.

In the last three years, she has been more sedentary than she ever was, for she has been doing more mind research and less walking, and so she has lost part of her balance, and we wish her to do more walking and more water.

But this one is very stubborn, and because she has lost her balance in her weight, it is weighing on her mind and, as she is a human Jill, this is a point where she feels she is not worthy as our mouthpiece.

(Jill is overcome with emotion.)

We wish to bring this to the audience's attention to say we do not judge the outer. She may be less than perfect in many eyes as a human form on the outer, but we wish for her today to learn to be more accepting of self, and that's why we wish for her to be kinder.

A: Very good, thank you. We both seem to be out of balance, and a lot of people seem to be out of balance right now because things are so unusual. Everything is changing.

All of these changes that are happening around the world, are they meant to be happening?

J: *Without change, there can be no progress, for if a stream stops running and a row of rocks are placed across its pathway, that water will stagnate. And so it is with humanity.*

They have been on a treadmill, going round, and round, and round, and they have been stagnating. They have been like magpies, collecting shiny, bright objects, filling up the nest, and now the nest is so full there is nowhere to rest.

A: So, we all need to start making changes in our life. Very good.

J: *We wish for a declutter of the physical and the mental.*

A: So, I know how to declutter in the physical; I've been doing that for several months now. What is the best way to declutter the mind?

J: *We spoke to this one over the weekend about the peace train. How many carriages is the peace train carrying? Are they all loaded full of passengers, or are they empty and ready for the new?*

Many have problems with family members at this time, for many are receiving the vibrations, and their photonic structures are changing, and yet the family members that are not listening to the transmissions and are stagnant with the old are causing frictions and frustrations for many, for there is a cross-communication.

So, the Earthlings lie in bed and think about those that they are no longer aligned with and so there is no peace within, and so the mind gets cluttered with those thoughts.

So, we suggested to open the communication, say what's in your heart with kindness, no manipulation, and then let it be, but let it out, so it no longer inhabits the mind.

A: Very good. So, we need to get rid of those thoughts that are just rushing around in our mind in a nice way?

J: *Well, Alba, this is why you are not sleeping at night, for you have embraced this mission as this one has, so both of you are now busy bees. Also, Alba, we have lifted your photonic structure.*

You are not the same being as you were before. Your vibrations are running at a higher level. Therefore, you do not require the same amount of sleep, but we would suggest that you take a nap when you feel the need.

A: Thank you. I'll try to take that nap. Thank you about that. So, Jill was given some words which seem very strange for us today. This discourse is a little different. We were given the words resolution or re-solution, with a hyphen. What does that mean? Re-solution?

J: *This comes back to the word about decluttering of the minds; what is the solution?*

What does one need to say in order to get a resolution to the problem? Many humans have many problems, but what is the resolution?

What solution do they want to put to that particular problem? For the old ways are no longer working. We wish new pathways now to be forged. So there needs to be new solutions, for the old energy has not been serving any of you.

It is time for a collaboration of many. Many now need to come together in small pockets and assimilate with each other to get resolutions and solutions to what is troubling them in their communities and in their families and talk it out.

We do not wish any festering to be inside these human bodies at this time, for this only leads to dis-ease within.

A: Now, during some of the gatherings that I do, we do something like that in groups, where they themselves get together and help each other come up with that resolution of their own issues. Is this something similar to what you're talking about, getting together in groups and just allowing that person to work things out?

J: *We see the groups, and we see the healing that is taking place, but each person has to own that themselves. They have to come up with their answers themselves.*

The problem that so many humans have is that they like to play what you call the blame game. They blame somebody else for the lack within, for it is easier to cast a stone against another than to look within and do the work, and this happens due to lack of self, self-value, value of self.

For when one realises one has value, then one wishes to clean up one's act. Every time that you see somebody playing the blame game, or play the victim, it is because they have forgotten who they are.

They have forgotten that they have come on this Earth domain in order to experience what they term the good, but the bad as well. For they have come here to experience duality, have they not?

A: Yes.

J: *So, that's why we say it is a time to go within, for we have already held a session called self-examination.*

A: Yes.

J: *When one examines oneself, then one finds the clutter, and as long as one has clutter, then one drags oneself around each day. As this one every day thinks about what she is putting in her mouth, for she knows she's most unhappy with self, dragging her physical weight around, and it weighs heavily on this one, and yet she insists on giving herself treats.*

A: Well, they do taste good.

J: *And yet it continues to weigh heavily, such is the human nature.*

James and I are having a smile at this one. She wishes for a lighter load, she speaks about a lighter load for many, and yet she doesn't treat herself with kindness. It's time for this one to declutter, Alba.

A: So, who's going to help her with that?

J: *Her husband.*

A: Wonderful.

J: *Last night she put out a cheeseboard. He wanted the cheeseboard, but he declined but watched her, she helped herself to the cheeseboard and when he deemed she had had enough, he thought he was being subtle as he wrapped up the cheese and put it away.*

She knew well that this is his way of helping her not to have another piece of cheese. So, she smiled inwardly, for he was showing great love, but he felt he couldn't say anything to this one, for he did not want to upset her.

A: That's wonderful. You know, in these times when you talk about getting together and helping each other, a lot of people are feeling isolation, and it's a good time for reflection, but sometimes when you talk things out it helps.

Just like before we got on this call, Jill and I talked things out. What would you tell those who are out there that are on this spiritual journey that are so lonely and don't have people to talk things out with and resolve their issues?

J: *This one has been working behind the scenes with a few others in order to set up a new portal for those who need to make contact with others for what you deem emotional support.*

Alba, we believe that in the next two days you will be given this new portal, and able to advertise it, and it will reach many, those alone dwellers, and although many dwell with others, they too are alone and feel alone.

But we are here for them all, for all are guided and it is time for them to now reconnect and align within themselves, their higher selves, and us.

A: Great. What is this exit gate that you wrote about?

J: *We are showing her the exit gate. It is through hyperspace. It is a portal of immense depth. We are setting it up. It's a new structure for the exit gate for ascension. It's being put into place.*

A: Okay. You know the last session we had, the last discourse, or two of them ago? You talk a lot about the leveller and the ascension, and there's a lot of people who are very confused about what this levelling is all about, and this ascension.

Can you take a moment now to review this again, because you've shown us an exit gate now that's going to scare people even more. Can you talk about what's happening?

J: *We wish humans to have a deep understanding of whom they are, for did we not say that they are light beings? And what is a light being?*

A being is an energetic form, this energy transverses throughout the multiverses, changing its photonic structure. Humanity is on Earth at this time to assist Gaia with ascension.

In order for ascension to take place, the boulders have to be removed from the river in order for the stream to run back to its home.

At the moment, Gaia is being stagnated. She is not running smoothly, she needs release. When she is being held down, she is unable to ascend. She needs to lose a load and shift her vibrations in order to rise.

Many changes will be arriving. We do not wish humanity to fear, but we would like to get back to the word clutter.

We wish for them to be lighter, not filled with clutter, for the clutter is what is holding them back and holding them down. They need to rise above, and they need to rise with Gaia because the great leveller will come for all, for Covid is part of the great leveller, for are not all affected equally?

A: Yes, absolutely everyone.

J: *Man, woman child, all nations, all creeds, all religions. It is a leveller, and how are they faring?*

A: Oh, equally. Everyone is the same, everyone's feeling it.

J: *Are not some more contained in self than others?*

A: Oh, yeah, there are those who are very grounded and spiritual, and those understand. But everyone is affected equally, in one way or the other. Either by the way the world is feeling, you could just feel it, in the atmosphere.

J: *All were created equal. All have choices. All came to experience. And yet they forget who they are. Then they blame another for their experience, for what it is that they chose. It is time for self-examination, it is time to go within, it is time to quieten the mind, it is time for the rivers inside themselves to run again, to be fresh, to be invigorated. Let out the stagnation, for no one holds it within you but self.*

So:

If one wants turbulence, then one chooses turbulence.
If one chooses calm, then one has calm.
If one gives out energy, one receives energy.
What is it that you wish to feel?
What is it that you wish to experience?
Are you going to be the ambulance, or are you going to be the siren?

A: I've a question about these changes that are happening because I'm noticing that a lot more people are developing their "claire's" now, at this time; clairaudience, clairvoyance, they're beginning to channel light language, they're beginning to experience things they didn't experience before. Is this part of the changes that are coming through?

J: *This is what we term "the change-over."*

A: Can you tell us about that?

J: *They are changing over their structure. We are showing this one flipping a coin, heads and tails, and what was tails is now heads, or what was heads are now tails. They are seeing another side, for if you do not take the coin off the table and flip it, how will you see the other side?*

A: Yes.

J: *So many now are embracing their missions, as are you and this one, and their true nature is rising to the occasion. For as you and this one are reaching many, so they too reach many, and it's apt that you term the language, or the communication, or the vibrational tone, light language, for we find this amusing, for every Earth being that communicates daily is using light language, for they are light beings.*

It is their structure. So, one who now is using light language is reconnecting with their sovereign state, with their star-seeded lineage. Their ankh, Alba, is activated.

A: Wonderful, now one of the things that came into my mind while you were speaking about that is that all of these people who are waking up. When you think of the whole population of the Earth, how many of us are supposed to wake up at this time?

J: *As many as are needed for our tipping point.*

A: Okay, so will everyone wake up eventually, or only a few?

J: *No, those ones that are not waking up at the moment, those ones that are causing consternation with families, we would like now to put in the listener's mind that of a boat, and the ballast that, at the bottom, that holds things. There are many that are holding. We said each being that came here at this time came here to assist with ascension. Some are holding, some are ready for the next step, and each graduate at their own time.*

A: So, what about those who are rocking the boat?

J: *They have a job to do. They need to rock the boat, for those other ones will approach and be the ones that will steady it, will regain the balance, for what will their job be if they are not called in to steady the boat? It is the perfect analogy, Alba.*

A: Somebody must have given it to me. You guys keep putting pictures in my mind. I have to talk about them.

J: *We are giving you a chance to speak this session, Alba. We did hear your comment last time. What is it you wish to say, Alba?*

A: Oh, you caught me off guard now. I'm still seeing the guy rocking the boat.

J: *Alba, we turned up your volume, and we would like to incorporate you into our session. This one is feeling the vibrations through her body now. We would be honoured if you shared your connection this day.*

A: Thank you. One of the things I came up with is that recently my sessions have been home runs, they've been out of the park, they've been amazing. I've been connecting with people that have been experiencing a lot of things, and I feel so honoured to be able to assist them and, you know, I feel that this mission that I'm on, just like Jill when I first started, I felt it was too big of a mission. I said, "Why me?"

That was always the question — why me? Why am I the one that has to be the mouthpiece or the awakening? How did I get involved in all of this?

J: *We brought you together from your star planet as an original star seed with this one, as part of the ancients, and then the Egyptian era, the Essenes and your Peruvian encounters.*

You as a Sasquatch, many different incarnations, and the home tribe is coming home, for this is one of our biggest missions, and you will be hitting many balls out of the park, for all your grand-children are gathering. The seeds from many incarnations are coming back to the pod and then the pod will open, and all that knowledge will be transmitted.

This one is seeing a very, very, bright light with impulses (Jill demonstrates this with her hands) *like this huge wall of light, and it's just going absolutely everywhere, as it has been ordained.*

We wish humanity at this stage to love themselves, to embrace their loved ones, to pat each other on the back. If they have nobody to pat themselves on the back, then they must pat themselves on the back. For we would like to applaud them, we would like to congratulate them, we would like to thank them for coming at this difficult time to be part of the pulse, of the light, the All That Is.

Embracing, aligning, enjoying, living, dying, for when one takes one's first breath, it is ordained that one will take a last breath, and as they say on Earth, what is it that one is doing between the first breath and the last breath?

We do not wish the Earthlings to know when the great leveller arrives.

A: Well, thanks for reading my mind.

J: *For all wish to know, for all wish to be prepared, for we say, why is one not preparing today, why does one wait until tomorrow?*

This one tells herself daily, "Today, I'm only going to eat ABC", and she wakes up the following day and says, "Today, I'm only going to eat ABC," and so it is with humanity.

They put it off, and they put it off, but they want to know when the great leveller is going to arrive.

Alba, if we told humanity that the great leveller is coming in two days, what will they do? If we told them that it was coming in two months' time, what would they do? If we told them that it was coming in two years' time, what would they do?

What would their plans be? Why are their plans not such that if the great leveller arrives in one week, why are they not putting their plans in place now?

That is our strongest message for this session; prepare

yourselves NOW.

Did we not say to watch your words, for as you give to one, you give to self?

Did we not say to clear out and be clear as crystal, for the day of judgement is arriving?

Did we not say they are all particles of light from the All That Is, and all is perfection, and there is nothing to fear?

A: You've said all that.

J: *We have said all this, and yet they still want to know when the great leveller is arriving. What will they do with that information that they are not currently doing?*

A: Yep.

J: *We want them to be like a girl guide —*

1. **Be prepared**. *Prepared in self — we wish self to prepare self for self, for no other than self.*

2. *For this is each soul's incarnation, each soul's journey, no other.*

3. *This is self-first, clean self out.*

4. *It is not your job to clean out another.*

5. *It is your job to live this 3D life to its fullest, to your full capacity, and that's where the discontent creeps in, for many know they are not living to their capacity.*

6. *It's now time for capacity building.*

7. *Looking to self, heal self, and then others will be the reflection.*

Alba, we cannot be clear enough about this.

A: Beautiful, thank you for that. Who are we speaking with today?

J: *James.*

A: Thank you, James. James, what would you like to call this session?

J: *We are going to be very facetious and call it "Self-Examination Two." We would like to call this session "Doubt."*

A: Okay, she will get some more emails on that. Thank you, James, for all of this. Is there anything else you would like to say, or do you feel this session is complete?

J: *This one is very tired, so we wish for the doubt to be removed, but we doubt that it will. So, therefore, we feel a shorter session is very apt today, we are complete.*

A: Thank you, James.

CHAPTER NINE (Session 421)

THE SESSION

In this hypnosis session we continue our discourse as Jill channels Melchizedek and James. The session focuses on the Merkabah and the lightworkers here on a mission. We discuss children's education, the Annunaki and how Earth changes will disclose our past.

J: *The lift door is made out of rainbow plasma, it's shimmering with all the colours that you would find if you had to blow bubbles and they were trapped by the sunlight, and it senses when it's ready for you to exit, and then it looks like a runway, like a metal runway that's going into space.*

It is the same width of a ramp that you would use for a fashion show, so it's that wide, and it's got lights. Oh, my gosh, it's got crystalline light bodies all the way on either side, Oh, it's a guard of honour; they're welcoming me home.

A: Beautiful, what do you look like?

J: *I've got a very soft flowing robe on, I'm quite tall, I'm very masculine, actually. Although I feel masculine, they're using the word, genderless, though it has male aspects, and I've come back to take my place next to the All That Is.*

A: Wonderful, what happens next?

J: *It's quite funny. It's a quintessential image of sitting next to God, with all the white clouds billowing all around you, and it's as if the very sun is behind us, and there's just glory everywhere. There's just the brightest, brightest, light, and there are millions and millions and millions and millions of souls in front of us, legions of souls, and these are the light-workers, and it's God's light, or source's light, that's just pouring through all the vessels.*

A: And what is your role there? What do you do?

J: *I'm Commander in Chief, I'm in command of the light army* (Jill is emotional.)

A: It seems that this is a very important day?

J: *Yes.*

A: What's happening right now that you've called all of these light-workers?

J: *It's a call to arms.*

A: Tell me more about this.

J: *It is a time for the balance to be restored. The All That Is set up duality, like a chessboard, so each would have a place and time, and the dark and the light, and the light and the dark, and it has been unfolding for centuries, but now it's time for light to prevail, so we're setting up the chess game, we're putting everybody in place for the final charge.*

A: How does one know, as a light-worker, where they need to be on this chessboard?

J: *Alba have you not felt the pull?*

A: Yes.

J: *So, it is… it is an internal structure. It is an internal light beam, it is a catalyst, and it is an alignment. Did we not say, in our last session, that the humans must stop filling themselves up with dross at this time, in order to receive the communication and the guidance that they need for ascension?*

A: Yes.

J: *For this is a light brigade, and if you want to move forward with speed, you have to be accurate and light. Quick, like lightning, physically and mentally astute.*

A: I know you have talked about this before, but what is the best way to do this, for those who have not heard this before?

J: *There are many new seeds in the nursery. We told you in the very first session that we had with this one that her connections run deep. She is connected to the multiverses, and she is connected directly with source, and that is why her connections are so far and wide, for she has been sowing the seeds through the multiverses, through the star-seeded lineage, and they are here, and they are now sprouting.*

If they are listening to this transmission, if they are reading these words, they are part of the immediate team. These words will resonate with them, they will then tune in and watch all the other sessions, and they will gain much clarity.

A: Wonderful. Now, you talked about new beginnings with Jill. You wrote those words. What does that mean, new beginnings?

J: *On the first of January, in your Earth year, you have what is called a new year do you not?*

A: Yes.

J: *And do many humans not make many promises and set new goals on a new year?*

A: Yes, we call those resolutions, New Year resolutions, and most people don't ever fulfil those, they give up very easily.

J: *That is why we wanted to bring in the word new beginnings, for every day, as you awaken, it is a new beginning. What are you going to do with your new day? Is it going to be the beginning of something new, or are you going to keep totally ensconced in your old ways?*

The new energy that is coming needs to be affirmed with a freshness and a lightness of being. So, we don't want old beginnings, we want old endings and new beginnings. We don't want a resolve. Today is the day to get out your shovels and dig deep, for you need to be rooted, you need to be grounded, you need to know what it is you like, and what it is you dislike.

We gave this one the image of a baby yesterday and food.

Would you put candy into a baby's mouth?
Would you put soda into a baby's mouth?
Would you put alcohol down a baby's throat?
Would you let a baby vape and smoke?

If the answer to all of those are no, then why do you deem it fit for an adult's body, for this body, and this system is a human system, and anything that is artificial or chemically induced, is not the finest choice for the system, for your light body, but you have free will.

Do you wish to be a heavy traveller or a light traveller? The choice is yours. You who are listening have taken on a mission of light. It is now time to pull up your socks and get on with the work.

A: Many are going to ask, "But what is my purpose?" That is the number one question I get every single day, "What is my purpose?"

J: *It is twofold. There are only two items. The first one is to be true to yourself, and the second one, we spoke to this one about it last night. She had a very good friend who was in her eighties, called Clarice and she asked that friend, "At your time of life, what is it you can give me, as a gift of knowledge, for my life ahead?"*

At that stage, this one was in her early thirties. The old lady said, "There's only one rule that I live by. I treat everybody who crosses my path the way I would like them to treat me."

So, if you are true to yourself, which is who you are, which is your light vehicle, which is your light body, and a light being, you will then be pure of nature, and because you are pure, you will give out purity, and because you give the purity out, that is what you will receive.

So, therefore, her friend was correct, and her friend was much loved, for she was generous and gentle with all that crossed her path, and she was kind, and she was compassionate, and that is what she received in return. So, Alba, it is very simple.

A: Thank you. You spoke to her about Melchizedek and the Merkabah, can you explain what that's all about?

J: *She has the fractal of Melchizedek. We sent her to Earth as a*

Melchizedek, as our high priest, in order to show them and teach them about their light bodies, about their Merkabahs.

A Merkabah is what each and every one of you have. It is your true form, it is your energetic form, it is your two pyramids, and they are turning at incredible speed in opposite directions.

Inside is your magic square, and we have spoken of the structure before, when we discussed the cloaking of one's light body, in order to cloak the 3D body from those that enter the trap doors through our energetic fields, or field around your Earth plane, in order to protect you humans, our star-seeded lineage.

This Merkabah, how many people know about it? How many people feel it? How many people align with it? How many people treasure it?

A: I would say that only those people that are spiritually enlightened really know about this. Can you tell me more about this?

J: *Your Merkabah is who you are, it is part of your hologram, and she's seeing it now, she's seeing the pulses of light. You spoke about the rainbow warriors when we started this session, she told you about the plasma lift door, with all the rainbow colours.*

A: Yes.

J: *When you come into this Earth plane, you are guided and shown your colour, your wave of colour, which is your vibrational frequency, and so the rainbow warriors came under this one's guidance, as Commander in Chief.*

She orchestrated the kaleidoscope in order that the warriors carry different colours, different vibrations, and scattered them across your Earth plane so that each frequency would be vibrating in a particular area, for colours hold frequencies, and vibrations and different areas of your Earth plane have different densities.

I'm sure as your Earthlings travel across this plane, this planet, they will have a feeling inside that they will resonate with when they step off an airplane into a new place. Do they not feel the vibration of an area?

A: Oh, yes.

J: *When you go to Peru, as opposed to New York, would you say the vibration is the same?*

A: No, New York is much denser.

J: *If you went to Hawaii, or you went to Chicago, would you get a different feeling?*

A: Absolutely, and I have.

J: *And this is due to the vibrations that each area is giving off, and the particular humans give off that live in those areas. So, we managed to get what we termed street lights together, in human form, through their light bodies, and placed them in different areas, and we placed this 3D* (Jill) *in a place called New Zealand, and we pulled her out of her home base (in her current incarnation) in South Africa, for we needed her to be nurtured in an area where it was very safe, and where the frequencies were high, in order to do the work.*

A: I've often told those that I have gatherings with, they're placed in the darkest places because they are the light.

J: *And they often have the most tumultuous family upbringings.*

A: Why is that?

J: *Because they are the ones that hold the light. Alba, this one was drawn to wearing a crystal today, and we see you are equally attired.*

A: I have many crystals.

J: *We aligned you both today with crystals, in order to remind you of your crystalline structure, and so it was apt that you used the crystal city, for the humans that are here in their crystalline structures, they will radiate, they will pulse, and you said, "What is it that they need to do?" They need just to be.*

Do not listen to the discord from the exterior.

Be as a pillar of light, receive your communication, receive your guidance, love yourself, love another, for all are one.

The tempo is quickening, the orchestra is getting to that time in the musical piece where all the notes on all the pages are starting to get very excited. It is a time for increasing one's elevation. One's tone needs to be heard.

A: Wonderful. Now, you talked in previous sessions about this great levelling and the wave that's coming. Is this wave going to be affecting our Merkabah?

J: *Correct.*

A: Does it look any different, or does it move or pulse differently, with this wave?

J: *When you talk about it affecting your Merkabah, your Merkabah is the All That Is. So, it is either expanding or contracting. As the energy hits, that Merkabah is aligned, that Merkabah will decide if it's staying to hold the light and infuse with the energy, or if the energy is too much for that smaller Merkabah, then that Merkabah will vacate. It may rise, it may watch what's happening, and then it may decide to come down again.*

But the Merkabah will change its form, its energetic form, in a slight deviation of pattern. We are now showing this one a Chinese lantern. A Chinese lantern comes in a flat pack. When you open up the flat pack and pull the Chinese lantern up, does it not form a perfect form? But whether that Chinese lantern is flattened or whether that Chinese lantern is opened, is it still not a Chinese lantern?

A: Yes, it's a different form.

J: *So it is with the Merkabah.*

When we talk about the Merkabah changing form, the 3D form, its energetic form, is part of the Merkabah, which is housed within the Merkabah, within the magic square, that will change from incarnation to incarnation.

But the Merkabah will be like the Chinese lantern, flattening and then rounding out, flattening and then rounding out. It is your connection, it is your umbilical cord to the All That Is.

A: There is a passage in the Bible where it talks about the end of times. About one moment someone will be there and another moment they won't. Are we talking about something like this? Where the person is just in a different dimension? The Merkabah changes?

J: *We showed this one many years ago what looked like liquid rain, and when she looked at it more closely, it looked like mercury, or molten silver, or lead, and she was quite fearful, and she looked up, and she saw thousands and thousands and thousands of what you term spaceships, all in the sky, and we told her all the light-workers will be lifted in a nanosecond, that there was nothing to fear.*

A: Wow, is that what's coming?

J: *Aaaah, how do we answer this?*

A: I'm sure there's a lot of mouths that are dropping right now.

J: *This is a time for revolution, for there has to be a revolution in order for there to be an evolution, and the evolvement is about expansion, for the Earthlings have been contracted, they have been contracting themselves, for they did not know who or whom they are.*

The Earthlings do not know they have a Merkabah, and so we sent Melchizedek back to reach many, to re-engage with their light bodies, to change the system, to change the programming of old.

Your teachers in what you term schools teach you about the ABCs, but this does not ready you for life, and that is the system that has to change, for you are learning in a very antiquated, antiquated like antique, an antique way.

This system has been propagated for many, many years, but it does not serve humanity at this time.

Covid changed a lot; it was part of bringing in the great leveller, because many children were being taught from home, from their parents, from their caregivers, and they were looking at new things, watching the birds settle in the trees, looking at the butterflies, thinking about things, interacting with their brothers and sisters, their mothers and their fathers.

This interaction, this communication, is not taught at schools. They are even removing what is termed religion at many schools, and religion is different for everybody, but the religion they were teaching was biblical religion, which was also twisted in its day, but at least they were getting what is termed good old-fashioned values.

When we speak of education, we come back to the two items of being true to oneself and treating another as you treat yourself. As you would like to be treated, rather, because many do not treat themselves very well.

Where are the classes where they teach values?

Where are the classes where they study stars?

Where are the classes that are taught nutrition?

Where are the classes that teach people to honour themselves?

Now it's all on the external, the exterior. This one flicked onto what's termed the blue box (TV) *the other day, and flicked through the channels, and found a channel with what you call gyration, and it was nothing but sexual provocation, very little attire.*

She thought, any child of any age could be looking at this, and what is it actually teaching the child?

We don't say restrict everything, for everyone has a right of expression, but what we're saying is, if you teach all your children at a young age to honour themselves, how many will find it necessary to remove most of their clothing and contour their body into a certain way, and make jerky movements to attract attention to what is coming out of your mouth?

For us, we find this most strange behaviour, for if one has what you term soul, and you are a singer, why would you need everything else in order for your song to be heard?

A: So, as parents with children, this is what we should be focusing on at this time, to teach them values, teach them about the stars, teach them about nutrition, and how to honour themselves, and treat others like they would like to be treated. Is this what parents should be focusing on with their children?

J: *Parents should be taking the time to parent, but many parents are absent parents, through the systems that have been put in place in order for them to earn money to pay for food, shelter, and utilities.*

To buy things that they do not need, in order for them to feel good about themselves. The children, many of them are here to teach the parents. If the parents spent enough time listening to their children, they would find great wisdom.

But these children need to be taken out of their apartments, out of their houses, removed from the brick and mortar. They need to be with their parents in nature, they need to remove their shoes and socks and play in the mud, run on the ground, feel the grass, lie on the grass, fly a kite.

Children need fresh air, the sunshine for, like a plant, they grow better in nature.

But so many parents are so busy trying to earn enough money in order to what you term earn a living that they place them in front of the blue box. So, they are sitting in front of this television, and what is it that they are absorbing? The parents do not know, and we would like you to look at children's programmes and look at the subliminal messaging and the marketing that these children are experiencing.

It is time for the parents to be responsible, for there are many irresponsible parents. There are very many what you term poor children, who have very good parents, for they do not have the money for a blue box, for a television, so they are the children's entertainment.

Maybe it's time for these busy parents to actually make an appointment with their children.

They have to ask themselves, why did they give birth? Why did they have a child? And is it not child abuse, abuse of a child to not look after it properly?

But these young children that are coming in, coming with many abilities, they have come to hold the light, and they are part of the changeover.

The changeover from the old to the new. For it is time for the crossing, and we wish many listening today to look up and see what the crossing means.

Have a look in your night skies; there will lie a few answers. Christ was on the cross, and this was very symbolic, for he was to come back at the time of the crossing, and so we are now at a crossroads.

Those that are listening are saying, "C'mon, c'mon, give us the answer. You haven't answered Alba's question. We want to know, is this the end of times?" And what would you do with that knowledge? Will you panic? Will you pack? Will you make changes? What would you do if this one told you that the end is near?

We wish for you all, as we said, to drink more water, for when your cells are full, your guidance through your Merkabah to your cells will be full, and you will be guided where to go and what to do.

But all that are listening, including you, Alba, including this one, has an expiry date.

Some are short, some are long, all have come to hold the light for a certain period.

Be well.

We are with you.

We salute you all.

A: Thank you. Can you tell me why the word trust, came up?

J: *We gave this one the word trust just last night. This one hasn't trusted herself, this one has been nervous, for every single session. She felt she wasn't enough, she doubted herself. She couldn't understand why we chose her as our mouthpiece and, in the last session, we said that we will not let her down.*

She has only just listened to that session, and for the very first time, she is realising what it is to be who she is, which is not a 3D, but a Merkabah, a cell in the All That Is.

Therefore, she now has trust, for she knows she has done this many times, not only on this Earth plane but throughout the multiverse.

So, you have supplication, which is called faith, faith in the afterlife, but we want you to have faith in this life.

Trust that you are here, as a light being, holding the light, in the areas where you live. You are on a mission. Your life will be what it is.

There is nothing that can happen to you, for everything happens for you. For your choices will bring either contraction or expansion. Fear not, trust. Follow your guidance and enjoy this adventure.

A: Thank you for that. It seems like you're picking my mind.

J: *Alignment, Alba, alignment.*

A: Yes, thank you for that. I told Jill I was feeling like Noah. It seems like I'm on a mission. I just don't know when it's going to rain.

J: *Alba, you are on track.*

A: Thank you for that. Can you tell me a little bit...?

J: *We need you, Alba.*

A: What is it?

J: *We need you. We are guiding you. Have trust.*

A: Thank you, thank you. So, tell me about the Canaanite? She was woken from a dream with the word Canaanite, about the land of Canaan, I guess. Not sure how you say that.

J: *The reason that we showed this one about Kenite — and she pronounced it like that — she laughed when she thought of that because she thought of Ken and Barbie. She had to remember Ken and Barbie doll because, otherwise, she wouldn't then remember the name. And then she said Ken, Ken, Kenite, what does this mean? And then we put her thought process into Cain and Abel so that she would remember the Ken side of things.*

And so she remembered, and we would now like to say that we gave that to her because we wish her to look up Melchizedekian, part of Canaan and the Canaanites, part of the ancient family from Noah, and that is why we were very amused with your comments about Noah this morning, and hers with Melchizedek.

That's where the alignment is, Alba. She comes from that ancient lineage, as our priest of the highest, from the land of the Canaanites.

They migrated and ended up in what you now term Jerusalem, Salam, Salam, Salam, which then became Jerusalem.

A: Wow.

J: *Many need to study the history of where the light came from. Your session called "I am Freedom" is airing tomorrow. In that session, we spoke about nobody being above another, and yet you have on your Earth plane cultures and people who call themselves God's chosen ones and feel they are above another race. There was much light in that area.*

We want to say all who are on this Earth plane are God's chosen ones, for are you not a particle of the All That Is?

A: Yes.

J: *You all have expanded and travelled throughout time/space continuum, so that the All That Is can experience what it is? And that is why you have Tabaash that reminds you and says, "You are God."*

And many find this sacrilegious, but if you are a particle, a cell, a soul, out of the All That Is, then what are you?

This finger is a finger in the 3D body of Jill. This hand is a hand in the body of Jill, but is it not still part of the body? And does this body choose this finger, or this eye, or this mouth to be more important than another? For all of the pieces, the organs, the cells in this body make this body what it is.

So, all are chosen for the structure in order for the structure to be all that it can be for this particular incarnation. And so it is with all the people on Earth, the colours, the creeds, the nations, the little children, and the big children. All are loved equally. It is time for humanity to know who they are, to love themselves.

Alba, we made this one wear a crystalline heart today because we want people to connect with their hearts, what makes them feel. They need to connect with their feelings, and then they need to speak. You have what's termed a funeral, Alba. Is this not a place where you start telling everybody how fabulous that person was?

A: Yes.

J: *I mean, that person is dead!*

We would like funerals to be held while the person is still alive. What is stopping humanity from telling each other today what they would say at somebody else's funeral?

We want today to be a funeral day, a fun-eral. Let's make it a fun-eral day, let's make it lots of fun, let's lift the vibrations. Everybody listening to this transmission, you see how this one suddenly has become energised?

A: Yes.

J: *Because this excites her. This will help many with their self-esteem when they hear from another how those people in their lives feel about them. They will know then that their existence has worth and value.*

This one has much love for you. She does not always say it, she does not often express it. We are going to get her, after this session, to speak to you about her great love for you. For did she not remove her glasses for you alone when she was in Peru? Did you not see the emotion that this one held for you? (This happened when Jill started channelling in front of their soul family)

A: Yes, it was very emotional.

J: *For you and this one have had many, many adventures together. It is a time for vulnerability. It is a time for husbands and wives, and mothers and fathers, and children, and grand-parents to express themselves about those in their lives.*

This is a time of the quickening.
This is a time of the great leveller.
This is a time of the crossing.
This is a time when the trumpets are trumpeting.

The Commander in Chief is here for the light army, to bring the light to a certain point in time so that all the Merkabahs come together. All the vibrations, the frequencies, the patterns, the rainbows. This is immense power and light.

Let the party begin.

A: Wonderful. Was she creating some sort of machine to bring us all together because she was shown a blueprint of that? Is this where the party will be held?

J: *We are showing her* Star Wars, *and we are showing her the light saber, but the machine that she carries is an activation that you see in your pyramids in Egypt. It is the handbag.*

A: Ah. People always want to know what that handbag is. We now know what the wrist watch is. What is the handbag?

J: *This is an activator.*

A: Can you talk more about this? That came up in the Annunaki video.

J: *This is a fine tuner. This can change the weather patterns, like your chemtrails, like your harp* (Jill spoke one word but sound was not recorded) *like a laser beam, it can create sound waves. It has the ability to change photonic structure.*

This one is part of the ancients. This one had an incarnation, as Annunaki, key to the Anu, to the All That Is, Lord Galactic, Lord Almighty, Lord over us all.

The Annunaki also come from source. He bestowed upon them the gift of the handbag. In the human race, many of the females carry the bag. All their possessions are in the bag. Do not touch the bag, they say, do not look inside my bag, for there is great power in the bag. That bag was given to the gods of creation in order to create the photonic structure, working with the Merkabah's fine-tuning.

There's much for the human race to discover:

With the upheavals.
With the event.
With the great leveller.
With the crossing.
With the tectonic plates shifting.

New discoveries will be made, but they are very old, but they will be new, and so the Earthlings will then learn who or what they are, and how many have deceived them for many years.

For we showed this one what you term priests on your Earth plane, for this is the duality in all, Alba, the light and the dark in all institutions, in all corporations, in all bodies.

So, we showed her these high priests, with their collars, and the great leveller arrived, the great energy arrived, and the cloaks flew off. There was no longer a disguise. What they were doing was now exposed, for there has been a lineage for many years in what you term religion, of a suppression of the people, telling them rules and regulations in order to ascend.

For ascension, there are no rules, there are no regulations to ascend, for all are equal, all have free will and, as these Earth changes appear, old rock forms, information, will show the Earthlings the heritage of their lineage, of their star-seeded lineage.

This is now James speaking.

A: Thank you, James.

J: *My brother, Melchizedek, has been speaking. This is now James speaking. My brother, Jesus, Yeshua, has left evidence to say His people were here, and the training that He received through His light body, in the pyramid.*

This information will be found, Alba. Many will talk about it, there will be those that will want to take this information and hide it, as they have done with much information over the years. Do you not have classified information?

A: Tons of it.

J: *It is held…*

A: Too much.

J: *Why?*

A: It would be empowering to us if we knew the truth.

J: *So, when you have your peaceful sittings, the power to the people, for the people, of the people, when the people know who they are, will their placards say, Equality for All?*

Classified documents — is this equality for all? Are there those that deem to be above the people? That they are allowed the information, but the people who are paying them are not allowed the information?

We want things to be clean. We want things to be clear. We wish no deceit, no corruption. We wish for way-showers to be in governance, rather than leaders. It is time for the disclosure to begin. There is something called disclosure on your Earth plane, but we say be wary of that particular platform, for it is not what it seems to be.

A: Do you imagine that these words will reach those that are in leadership in order to make a change?

J: *We didn't want to say too much in this session today, and we are now treading a very fine line, for should the information reach those in governance today, there will be a shutting down of this one.*

A notification that this one received from Facebook last night said that from October, Facebook will be putting new procedures in place. This is because the powers that be can see where the light-workers are at. Is there not great agitation throughout your Earth plane at the moment?

A: Oh, yes, a lot of it.

J: *For we showed this one the revolution, starting in 2017, and so it has begun. Your media and your social media are now watching and aware. In times gone by, in the ancient times, when you had all the little hamlets, all the little villages, you had a priest in each area, and the person would go into a little closet, and they would reveal their sins.*

There are not many that are now attending what you term a church sermon, for life has been modernised. So, now that the governors in governance have not heard through the priest how the people are feeling, there is a new type of surveillance that has been put into place.

Call it Google, Snapchat, Instagram, Twitter, Facebook. Do not for one minute think that you are not being monitored, for your smartphones are the ears for the eyes that cannot see. But you are being entertained, and you are paying to be heard and seen.

A: Yes. Is there anything else you wish to tell us today, James?

J: *Yeshua watches over you all, as does our Father, as does Melchizedek, as do the disciples, many of who are now incarnated under this light army.*

The general is with you, Alba. The tribe is coming together. Fear not. The plan is running smoothly. The rainbow bridge, the exit portal, everything is being aligned. There is much work being done in the background. Our space brothers are in place, the fleets are hovering, the trumpets are ready.

Let the party begin.

A: Thank you very much for that. What should we call this session today?

J: *The Session.*

A: The Session.

J: *The Session.*

A: Sounds good to me. Thank you so much, and I look forward to seeing you again or talking to you again, next week. So, with that, I'd like for you to go ahead and...

J: *Alba.*

A: What is it?

J: *It is our pleasure and, once again, we would like to thank you, and today, through my brother, Melchizedek, and Jesus, and myself, we would like to thank the listeners for listening.*

They have a job to do.

This is a new beginning.

Pull up your socks, go and have a fun-eral.

We salute you.

We thank you.

We commend you.

Fear not.

All is in place.

We will soon be together again.

Let the fun begin.

CHAPTER TEN (Session 423)

ASCENSION

In this hypnosis session we continue the discourse as Jill visits the eighth dimension, the level of pure vibration. We are given detailed instructions on how to manifest and create the life we want. We discuss expectations, celebration, joy, and the importance of silence.

J: *And then I had lots and lots of... well, imagine if you are shooting bullets into a big steel door, but they don't penetrate the door, but they leave indentations. The indentations were facing me in the lift, and when I looked at the numbers on the lift, inside the lift, each one had a grid across it, and it was metallic, like a little mini cage, and the lower realms were one, two, three, and four, and they were all very, very, dark. As you get above level four, into the higher realms, it becomes lighter and lighter, and when you asked me to make my body dissolve as such, it felt strange, as my whole body became fluid, like water, until it was just a drop that was left inside the lift.*

But when I exited the lift, in 4046, that drop of water actually became pure energy, and it went like a, mmm, how can I describe this? Imagine if you are a fish put on supersonic speed, and your tail goes woosh, woosh, woosh through the water (Jill motions with her hands) well, that is pure energy, in rainbow colours, but it has fluid motion to it. So, all those colours, all that vibration, and all that energy was what took me straight into level eight, the eighth dimension, which is pure vibration. It's very, very, light, and it's an orchestra of sound waves, and there's nothing that's really dense there.

A: What are you doing and seeing in this dimension?

J: *Everything here is telepathic. It is… I'm being told the word, "pure creation." It's like you have experienced the depths of despair, all the darker worlds, and now you've chosen to experience a much lighter state of being. It's just different levels, like one, two, three, and four. So, right at the bottom, level one, or dimension one, it is just thick, thick, thick, like quicksand, tar, and a swamp, and one really struggles to move there. Everything's really dense, and then the levels of density change each time you get higher and higher. It's lighter and lighter, you have more ease, you can go to different places quickly.*

A: Yes, so what density are we in now?

J: *On Earth, Alba? Well, there's a changeover happening at the moment, between the fourth and the fifth.*

A: How can you tell the difference, whether you're on the fourth or the fifth density?

J: *It really depends how much is still holding you down, how much you're getting upset about things, how much you're able to view stuff that is playing out on your Earth stage, the way you watch your politicians, like little puppets.*

You get removed from it in the fifth, you have a greater understanding of the play. It's almost as if someone's given you the script. It's as if you go to see what you call a movie or a film; if you've read the book before you go and watch the film, you know what's going to happen. Correct?

A: Yes.

J: *So, you're watching the unfoldment of the story you already know in your head, but the actors look a little different. Maybe they're not exactly what you imagined in your imagination when you read the book.*

It is exactly the same when you start going into the fifth. You know the story, you know the book, but some of the actors are not looking, in your mind's eye, as to what you thought they would be. But because you know the story, it's not upsetting you as much, therefore, those that are going into the fifth are able to be what we term, of real use for the game ahead.

A: Okay, very good. Now you say that on this density, the eighth one, it is pure creation. What is creation? That was one of your questions; what is it?

J: *I really like that you got that in so quickly.*

A: (Alba laughs.) I'm getting good at this.

J: *Because, Alba, that actually should have been the very first question, because all the others come after that. Without creation, none of those other questions that we've put down today for you to ask would be able to be experienced, not so.*

A: Very good.

J: *So, we say 10 out of 10 to you today. You're coming along nicely.*

A: Thank you. I guess I have the playbook. (Laughing.)

J: *You've seen the movie.* (Laughing.)

A: So, what is it that we are creating, within and without?

J: *Alba, this one was told many years ago that humanity was created in order to create and with every living breath we ask, what is it that they are creating?*

For every choice that they make creates a new creation. It could be as simple as making a meal, meeting a new playmate, deciding whether to go with one particular person over another, to do something together.

For when they have choices, they have a new creation, and it is all in the thought process as to what one wishes to create. Humanity, in this fourth dimension, are very slow creators. As they reach the fifth, you have something called manifestation, that is what you've termed the new in-word, at the moment.

A: Yes.

J: *To manifest something, and then they think about abundance, just manifest it, and isn't this where the irritation comes in with humanity, because they want to manifest it, but they can't see it.*

A: Right.

J: *Right. It is because of their belief systems that hold them back from creating for themselves. We're showing this one now, those that you term, "in power."*

They are on the Forbes list, the rich list, world's most powerful. Tell me, Alba, how many brains do these powerful ones have?

A: Is that a trick question? Each one has their own brain.

J: *One brain, five brains, six brains?*

A: I guess it depends on how many there are on the list.

J: *If we talk about one human, do they have more than one brain in their skull?*

A: Just one.

J: *How many eyes do they have?*

A: Two.

J: *Do they have five arms, or do they have two arms?*

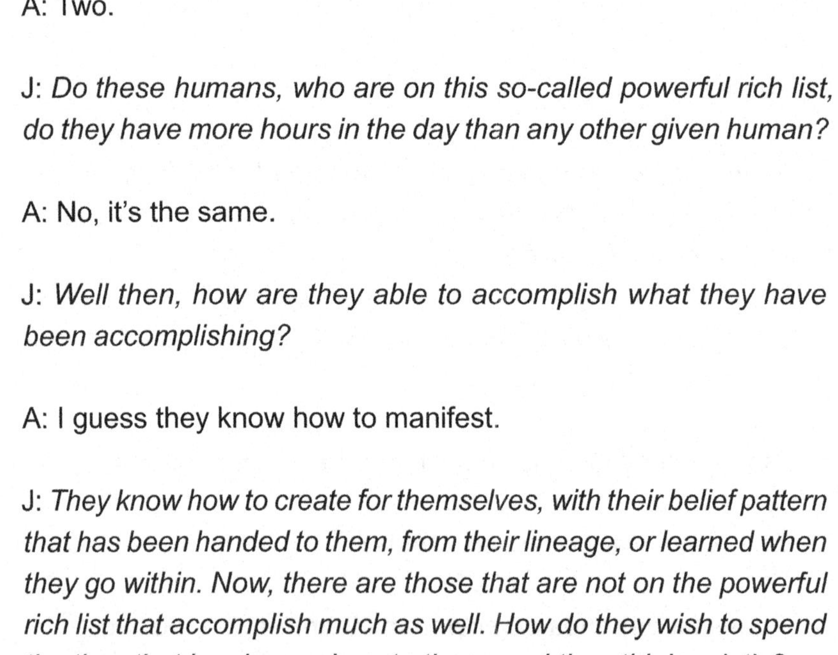

A: Two.

J: *Do these humans, who are on this so-called powerful rich list, do they have more hours in the day than any other given human?*

A: No, it's the same.

J: *Well then, how are they able to accomplish what they have been accomplishing?*

A: I guess they know how to manifest.

J: *They know how to create for themselves, with their belief pattern that has been handed to them, from their lineage, or learned when they go within. Now, there are those that are not on the powerful rich list that accomplish much as well. How do they wish to spend the time that has been given to them, and they think quietly?*

This one was just speaking to somebody yesterday about how to achieve something. Humans have dreams and desires, and what do they do with those dreams and those desires? Do they write them down, do they think it's impossible to achieve? We want them to write down their dreams and their desires. Get a piece of paper, write them down.

But we want them to work backwards. Instead of saying, this is what I wish to achieve, I'm going to put $5 aside, and then I'm going to get up half an hour earlier. We want them to actually go from the top of the goal that they have right down to the base, rather than from the base to the top.

We want them to write down what they already have, in order to achieve that goal. If they want to have clean windows in the house, they might already have their two hands that can put pressure against the glass and have the cloth, or the soft paper, or the towelettes for the job, they might already have the squirty stuff to go on the window.

But if the windows are too high, how are they going to reach the top? What is missing on their list? A ladder, or a taller person? So, they already have many of the aspects needed to achieve what it is they wish to achieve. We use that as a very easy example, and many Earthlings don't like to ask for help, Alba. When they ask for help, they feel that it is making them feel less than.

But as a human, when you are approached to help another and you have the ability to help another, not only is it good for the person to help them, but it's good for the helper.

So, we want humans to start asking for help, start thinking about what it is they wish to create. They might wish for more courage; they might wish for a good voice coach; it is not always money-oriented. There are many things that they are able to do.

This one read a book many years ago that she took out the library, but then they were going to live in Wanaka, and relocating from Auckland — the book had to be returned. But we wished for her to retain it, for we wished her to teach many what was in the book. She picked up the three books that she needed to return and walked into the library and returned the books.

She no longer had any books out of that institution. She returned to her car, and to her great surprise, one of the books she had just returned was sitting on her passenger seat. She couldn't understand this! Remember we told you, this one has had many experiences before; this is one of the experiences that she has not discussed with anyone as yet, for she had forgotten this. She thought, "I would really like to have this book, but what am I going to do, because this book is not my book, this book belongs to the library."

She left the book in her car, she went back into the library, and she said to them, "Could you please check my account as a library user? Do I have any books outstanding?" and they said, "No."

At that time, this human had very little money. She was a young housewife. Had it been the same human in the same situation now, she would have paid for it, and just bought it, but we gave it to her as a gift, for the book had duplicated.

The library had that book, and we gifted her another version, and we would like to give the audience the name of this book today. It is called Wishcraft. (The book mentioned can be found at http://wishcraft.com/)

This Wishcraft *book, helped this one with creation, creating who she is today, and so we gave her exercises to do which were in the book that we gifted.*

We would like the audience today, should they not have means to buy this book, to follow these instructions: If they can afford to, buy a good jotter, a good notepad, or a good solid hard covered book with empty pages, for this book or notepad will contain your heart, your hearts feelings, your desires, your creativity.

Step one: Write in detail the following exercise in your book.

What kind of a day would you choose to experience, if money were no object? From the very moment you wake up until you put your head on your pillow to go to sleep at night.

So, this one really embraced this task. She decided to describe the room that she would be waking up in. Big windows, lots of natural light, a soft sea breeze coming through, a fresh bowl of flowers, a little writing desk under the window, and a comfortable chair. Her bed was so comfortable. As you can see, she loves linen, soft white and cream. (Jill, whilst being hypnotised, is lying on a bed with a soft linen cover over her which she points to.) *It was fresh, it smelt like sunshine off a washing line. Her pillow moulded her neck and her head so perfectly. She got out, slipped on a pure cotton gown, walked on stone floors into her bathroom, where she had a very big bubble bath, and lots of natural light.*

She didn't need curtains because there were no neighbours but rolling green lawns all the way down to the beachfront. Because money was no object, she could have anything she liked for breakfast, and wear anything she liked. She chose comfortable slacks and a soft linen top. She was a natural beauty in her own element, she was comfortable in her own skin, for she had privacy, she didn't have to feel less than, and so she went into her kitchen, filled her bowl with fruits and yoghurt, for it was a sunny summer's day, went outside onto the patio under a big umbrella, with a dog by her side, and her husband, and watched the waves rolling onto the beach.

After that, she put on a big hat, and she was driven to town, so she didn't have to worry about traffic — for she had the luxury of imagination and creation — where she was taken to an auditorium. She had set up this project where many speakers could come into many auditoriums, and speak to the masses, and inspire the masses, and encourage them to be the best they could be. She was a philanthropist in her imagination, helping to spread encouragement, joy, excitement, and upliftment.

After the talk, she met some girlfriends, they went to an art gallery, and then they went and had lunch, where they shared much laughter. In the afternoon, she was driven back to the house and went for a long walk on the beach with her dog, just feeling the gentle sea breeze blowing through her hair, not a care in the world. It was very much the feeling of the film that you have called As Good as It Gets. *That kind of attire, that kind of house and desk and chair, just soft, gentle, comfortable, and warm.*

Then she had an early evening drink with her husband, and her children arrived. They sat out on the patio, having fresh, good, wholesome food as the sun was setting. After that, her and her husband went to bed, beautiful candlelight. And that was what she wrote for her exercise in great detail.

Step two: (We then got her to do the following as step two.)

On a separate page, we asked her to write what it was she already had, that she had created in her mind.

So, she wrote the following. That she had the bed, she had the sunshine, she had the fruit, she had the children, the husband, she had the ability to speak out.

She already had beautiful lunch with her friends, she went to art galleries. She had her many speeches in her mind, for every night, did we not tell you, Alba, that she has been practicing these talks for years in preparation, and she is just realising now as she tells you this how she now is speaking to the masses.

Jill got very emotional when she realised what she wrote all those years ago had materialised.

A: She's already doing it.

J: *Her creation has reached fulfilment. She has her candles, she has her flowers, she has her sunlight, what she does not have are the rolling waves on the beach.*

A: Or the bathtub. (Alba laughs.)

J: *She does not have the dog. The dog will come, and she can visit the beach. So, suddenly she realised when she did the second page how much she already has.*

Step three: All she had to do on the third page is write up all the elements that would tie it all together. So, this is the process that we would like humanity to follow. For as one releases one's creative juices in detail, we in the eighth dimension, in 4046, which is the creative side, where the juices are free-flowing, for there are no boundaries, we hear the desires, we see the desires and, depending on the emotion and the vibration that is braided in and woven tightly in alignment, then we, like that book that was so wished for, we then bring it into manifestation.

Now there is a human on your Earth plane that wrote that book called Wishcraft. *She is called Barbara Sher. She is on what you term YouTube. She is a no-nonsense person just like this one, and she says if you have no personality and no friends whatsoever you can still have the life that you wish for. If you're retired, and you haven't attended to yourself, or you've given and given to others, and now you think, what is it that I'm going to do?*

Barbara Sher set modalities and tasks in order for humans to get to know themselves, and at that time, Alba, this one set up a course — her very first course — and she called it "Your Time to Shine", and she was very clever because she went to specialists, a wine specialist, a person who sharpens knives, she went to an author, she went to an artist, a fashion designer, and she invited them to a small hall once a week for two hours to share their skills. She said to the participants, just bring a cup with you for tea, that she will supply all the paints, writing materials, and specialists, and the specialists were happy to go there and give up their time for free because it would open them up for business.

This one didn't want to make money out of it, for she wanted to rather help these people find themselves. She felt that it was their time to shine, and she knew that there were so many areas of interest and that one of those areas would perhaps interest them enough to spark something inside them. To have some creative juices running again, and remind them that they weren't just the *mother, father, brother, sister, granny, grandfather or the caregiver, that they could spend time with themselves. Although she was fully booked for the course, she only charged $10 per session.*

We are giving you this example so that many who listen can maybe incorporate this in their own area, which will get them interested in something, get them to meet other people, not only the specialists in the field but new people in their lives. As they will be giving, they'll be receiving.

This one never did that course, for she had what is termed a hysterectomy, and then shortly thereafter is when we gave her the knee problem, the operation, in order to stop her energy all over the show for the work ahead, and we moved her to Wanaka. But we gave that to her as a creative exercise, for her to realise what it is she can achieve. So, Alba, that is the creative creation on the external, combined with going internal, and putting them together. Does that answer your question?

A: Yes, but you know, it seems to me that if you do have a creation, there has to be some emotion to move the creation. One thing is just daydreaming about it, but another thing is actually feeling it. Can you talk about that?

J: *That's why we said you have to have the emotion aligned with the wish, and you have to have the strength of those combined because thinking on its own is not enough, so thank you for reiterating that. It has to be braided together because the emotion is key, it is the vibration, and the stronger the emotion, the stronger the frequency, which penetrates to the 4046.*

A: Good. I have an example. What if somebody is thinking of their dream, they've planned it out, they're excited about it, but something happens, maybe somebody pops a hole in their dream, and they get discouraged. What happens then, if you allow that bubble, that dream, to burst? Do the doors close to your creation?

J: *That's a very good thing to say, Alba, because does that not once again happen in self, with lack of self, and allowing others to steer one's vessel, one's ship? Is one not master and commander in control of one's own vessel? When you eat daily, you're no longer a baby.* ***You put the food on the spoon or the fork in your own mouth. You don't say feed me, feed me. So, if nobody is feeding you food, physical food, why would you allow them to feed you mentally or negatively? That is giving your power away****.*

So, this is why it is so important for people to know who they are. That is why, in our last session, we wanted them to feel their energy, their frequency, their bandwidth, and their colour wave. When they said, "I am" out loud, they didn't say, you are, and you are, and you are. They said I. They were claiming their fullness, the sovereignty of who they are. But too many humans spend too much time denigrating another in order for themselves to feel better than another, and we say, "No one is better or less than you, but rather different, unique, and just as fabulous as you."

Celebrate each other.

A: Wonderful. So, can we talk about celebration?

J: *Yes, Alba, you are the master of ceremonies today. Look how you are weaving in the script! So, celebration. We want that word to settle, and how does humanity feel when they hear the word celebration or celebrate? Isn't it an excitement? Something's about to happen, that is a celebration.*

A: Yes.

J: *So, during this time period called Covid with all the demonstrations and unrest, how much celebration is going on at the moment, Alba?*

A: Not much.

J: *Not much. This is why we decided to bring in the word celebrate, and celebration today. You are still breathing; it is a time to celebrate the breath. When you wake up in the morning, look at yourself in the mirror and say, however corny it may sound, say,*

"I celebrate you."

You're standing up, or you're sitting in your wheelchair, you're still alive, you're a vibrant, creating human, and that is enough to cause a celebration. We spoke the other day about being prepared or getting ready for the great leveller, or the energy that is coming. We wish you on a daily basis to prepare, not only for the great leveller or the energy, but prepare yourself for yourself, and celebrate, because when you celebrate, it brings you to the eighth dimension, to the 4046, because it lifts you higher. When you mention the word Covid, there's a heaviness, when you mention the word celebrate, like celebration, like acceleration, it lifts you higher.

We want humans to do one little nice thing for themselves every day, in order to celebrate themselves. Look at their loved ones. When last did they turn to their loved one and say, "I celebrate you"? Just like we said in the last session, about the fun-eral, Alba, how many people celebrate the joy with another, other than their birthdays?

A: Well, I guess it depends if you go to happy hour or not. (Alba and Jill share a laugh.)

J: *Well, there are many ways of celebration; they are having a human experience.*

A: That's right. When you're with your friends, it's a way to celebrate, when you haven't seen each other for a while. Now people are doing celebrations on Zoom, where they get together with family and friends.

J: *That's a frequency isn't it? They are connecting on your waves, your airwaves, and they are connecting your frequency with their frequency, so it is a time of celebration for the nation. For there are many nations at the moment at war, but there are many humans that are at war with themselves. They look at the mirror, they do not see the perfect image that has been sold to them in the magazines, in the media, and then they feel less than. They do not see a cause for celebration, and yet that is the form that they chose to experience their humanness, their humanity, in this adventure.*

So, they need to look at the mirror, and think to themselves, why did I choose this particular energy form? What have I learnt from my perfections and my imperfections, and my disabilities? For there are many humans with what you term afflicted with disabilities. But these are not an affliction, for they have not only taught themselves so much, they have taught those that are living with them with these "afflictions."

A: So, how do you love yourself when you compare yourself to other people who don't have afflictions, or they have what you think is the perfect body or the perfect face? What do you have to say about that, since we do have to live a human experience?

J: *Alba, what is perfection to one is not perfection to another. Do you not have many nations on this Earth plane?*

A: Yes.

J: *If you were not Japanese or an Eskimo, or what is termed an African, or a Red Indian, or a European, how would you know what it is that they term perfection in their eyes? For what is perfect for them is imperfect for you. So, each nation, each culture, each creed, have been given a set of expectations of what it is to be perfect. We need to take you back to the previous conversation, Alba, where we asked you about whether you cared whether your friends were fat or thin, whether they have a straight nose, or a crooked nose, big ears or small ears, you don't love them any less.*

A: No.

J: *So, how do we teach humanity that they are acceptable, not only to us but for themselves? For the way humanity has been programmed is what's called false achievement, celebrating the fastest, the quickest, the strongest, the richest. That is a form of entertainment, that is not perfection, for in the All That Is, each one of you is perfect. Perfectly formed, perfectly loved, just the way you are, in your current form, whether you have freckles, pale skin, darker skin, black hair, brown hair, red hair, blonde hair, no hair, straight hair, curly hair, fat, thin, no arms, no legs, small breasts, large breasts, small stomachs, round stomachs.*

It's an energetic form, you are an energy form. What do you want to do with your form? What do you wish to create? What do you want to exude out of you, out of your essence, your heart? The feelings that you feel as a human about another human is how you feel about yourself, for have we not said before, when you see imperfection in another, it is because you see imperfection in yourself? So, we come back to creation again, Alba.

When humanity starts to create the life that they love, the person they love becomes more loving to self, for then there is an excitement, there is a focus, there is a purpose.

Alba, this one that does hypnosis sessions just like you do, she's noticed the number one question that every client wants answered is "What is my purpose?" Is that correct?

A: Yes, it is the number one question.

J: *Because they want to know that their life has worth. We would like each human listening to this transmission that if they are listening, they have been deemed worthy, and that is why they are breathing. They have worth, their purpose is just to be. Anything else is a bonus and worth celebrating.*

A: Wonderful, thank you. You had put something on the list which was very interesting, and it had me wondering about expectations — of ourself and others. That perhaps they were set up before we were even born.

J: *These expectation Alba. Humans have a period of nine months while they are being grown in this research centre, in this laboratory. What are the expectations placed on that unborn child? Even before the child, that baby, is born, there are mothers in the family, either the mother or the father, or the grandparents, or the siblings, that wish for that particular baby to be of a particular sex. "Oh, no, we don't want another girl." "Oh, we really need a boy to carry on the family name." "What a disappointment it's going to be if it isn't what we wish for." "Oh, this family has had winemakers for the last three centuries. We hope that this child is going to carry on being a winemaker."*

In actual fact, it is not a hope, it is an expectation that this is what this child is going to be. This is what this child is going to do, this child better not disappoint, and so we ask the question, disappoint who?

The yoke is placed by the love of the immediate family to be, to act, to become something other than perhaps what it desires, so the internal conflict starts within this being, for they do not wish to disappoint. For this is a very big trait in humanity, not wishing to disappoint or let down others, because they always have expectations. Often the expectations are not voiced, it is voiceless and yet one is very aware.

Some fare better than others, some remember that their voice box resides in their voice box and so they speak up and say, "I'm going to be an artist; I don't wish to be a winemaker." Now, there are those who are more astute than others, the parents, the winemaker parents, who then support that child to be all that they can be, to be the best being. And yet there are others that say, "Well then, if you're not going to be the winemaker and you want to be the artist, go and support yourself, let us see how you cope then." So, where is the love there? This is what we term conditional love. "Yes, you can be anything that you want to be, as long as it's what I want you to be."

A: There's a lot of that.

J: *And then what happens to this container, this vessel, this human? There's now no longer an ease within the system. The system becomes diseased. There are many listeners today who resonate with this.*

But this is not a blame, for they chose those players on the stage, this Earth stage. They discussed the scene before they arrived with the other light-workers, the light beings to assist them, to push them, to develop what is termed a backbone, to stand up for themselves.

There are many support players on the stage to bring out the greatness and the creativity that each of you hold within, and many blames another for holding one down, or not allowing you to do something.

It is fear that keeps you in a position that you do not wish to be, and so you blame the other, but when is one going to look at self and self-responsibility, for what is it that gives one joy and a cause for celebration?

Is it not freedom to be who you are?

But you have now been taught you need to be perfect; you need to be strong; you need to be quick; you need to be a certain way. Expectation after expectation after expectation.

So, whose expectations are you going to live by? Your own, or another?

We do not want you to have an expectation of self, we want you to embrace your desires.

A: Wonderful. Can you tell me about joy? What is joy?

J: *We bow unto you today, Alba. Your presentation of the items that we presented to you today are coming at the perfect moments.*

So how does one have joy in one's life if one is living for another's expectations? Then the joy of the breath, the joy of the life is robbed from one.

When one feels not enough and one is living for another's expectations, then the joy is not there. This one did a hypnosis session on a human yesterday who had had many, many moments robbed from her as a very young being, she felt "there is no life left for me. Why am I here? Why are these things happening to me?" and she learnt that nothing happened to her, everything happened for her, and she was the perfect example of a human that has been suppressed and rejected by so many. Used and abused is the terminology, and yet she rose above, for she came as a joy germ, spreading the joy like a beacon of light. She didn't play victim; she didn't embrace that, for she still found the joy.

Why? Because she found the joy in self waiting to come out.

What is joy? Just own yourself, and when you do that, that is what gives one so much joy. For when you own yourself, no one else can own you, for you came in as a pulse of light to shine, to transmit, to be all that you can be, to radiate, and it is a joy, is it not, when you hear a baby laugh? Why do people love to hear babies laugh and laugh and laugh?

A: It's pure, it's real.

J: *It's free. Do they care when or where they laugh?*

A: No.

J: *They just give of themselves in the moment. We want people to feel the joy that a baby feels, the way a baby releases themselves. The way a baby and a toddler see everything that is new, or parents, new parents with toddlers, they start learning about their environment all over again. The joy of a butterfly looking down at an ant or examining a worm, watching the birds in the sky. Suddenly, are they not aware of their world? And this is what we wish for humans.*

Rediscover the joy within, embrace it and radiate it out.

A: It's very easy to just own yourself when things are going well. These are tough times right now. People have lost their jobs, people are confined to their homes, people are seeing others very angry. What would be a quick way for you to focus in on this childlike world and get that joy back?

J: *If they can't afford bubbles like a child to blow, we want them to put some washing up liquid in the sink, froth up the bubbles as a reminder that that is who they are. They are light beings. How do they feel, Alba, when they are on the first, second, third, fourth rung, as opposed to claiming their place five, six, seven, eight? They have the ability to rise above any situation, and when the going gets tough, we don't want the tough to get going, because they are not tough. This is when they are vulnerable, they feel alone, this is when they need to connect their vibration with another, for the other's vibration when it touches this vibration, it will be able to hold it steady. For did we not say this is a time for chain-building? You need to be links on a chain. We wish for friends who notice those that are depressed to help them regain the alignment.* (Jill demonstrates this with her hands).

A: So, is this where the prince on a white horse comes in?

J: *Well, that is actually linked to expectations, marketing, profiteering.*

A: Tell me about it.

J: *Many disappointments, Alba. This one doesn't watch much TV any more but last night we got her to watch a show and she couldn't believe what she was seeing, and it was called* "A Farmer Finds A Wife."

She saw eight women, all different, all standing in a line, waiting for this one man to decide if they were good enough. And this is what you call entertainment? The one that is chosen out of the line has a feeling of elevation, but what happens to the ones that are not chosen? How are the emotions impacted on those ones? She couldn't help but think a farmer is finding a wife, and they could just as well be heifers! Are they going to be good breeders? What do the udders look like? Were the legs strong? Is this really entertainment?

One of the participants, who was 24 years of age, said, "Oh, I love him. I just want to marry him and have his babies." This 24-year-old two weeks prior had never set eyes on this human in her life, and yet now she's professing a deep love for him.

What has humanity come to? That this is now a form of entertainment for participants to get paid in order to make a mockery of emotions.

Little girls get taught that one day they're going to get a flowing dress, all white and sparkly, with a sparkly ring, and live happily ever after. This handsome man is going to come in and rescue you from your life and look after you.

When this doesn't happen and reality sets in and the dis-ease sets in, then what? And the men have expectations that their wife, their future girlfriend, is going to look a certain way. Do they not have apps called Tinder – swipe left, swipe right, depending on a photograph, whether they are going to pursue that being? They are being set up, manipulated, marketed and sold to.

If you speak to many women and men today who've been married for many years, and you said to them, "Would you have your wedding day again the way you had it then?" many would say, "No, we wouldn't have spent all that money on that big white wedding just for show. Although it was a fun day, in actual fact we could have had an equal amount of fun had we had it on a beach, put up a little canopy, or brought a plate of food." Because this is a celebration of two people loving each other, it is not about the show. Weddings are getting more and more ostentatious, and the pressure is building on the youth of today.

It once again comes back to expectations. "Wow! Look at the size of the ring. He must really love her!" Love has got nothing to do with the size of a ring, the sparkliness of a wedding dress. Whether they arrive on a white horse or not. It is nothing but a fairy tale that has been taught to you in order to market you and manipulate you.

Do not live beyond your means.
Do not live on the plastic credit cards.
Know that you are enough.
Food, shelter, warmth, love, friendship, family.
Humans need very little.

Most that is on the exterior is for those who feel inferior, and we love what Forrest Gump's mother said; "Forrest, you need very little. All the rest is for showing off."

A: Very good, thank you for that. What about the sounds of silence?

J: *You know, Alba, why people sigh? It's a letting go. When they do a meditation, they're taught to take a deep breath and release, and then once one has released, one has silence.*

When one has silence then one is truly communicating with self. For one cannot hear self with all the external noise. When one wishes to create, then one goes into silence. Ask any artist or any sewer. Ask anybody doing anything creative while they are busy in the middle of their creation. They are only concentrating on the next step, on each step. Their mind is not going elsewhere, because that is being silenced, they are living in the alignment of the moment.

We wish for silence for all, for their sacred days, for their sacred moments, to hear the guidance that is there, ready and open from the eighth, from the seventh, from the sixth coming through to the fifth, getting murkier to the fourth.

As soon as they go silent, they lose the distractions, and they open up the path of communication. This is when they learn to love themselves, accept themselves. They don't worry about expectations any more. They don't worry about the white knight, or the rider on the white stallion, the perfect girl, the perfect life, the high achiever, for they know who they are when they open in silence to receive.

A: Wonderful. I know that everybody asks, "What is my purpose?" But they all always ask how do I connect with my guides, with my higher self? Is that what you just said to them?

J: *Correct. You know you got something called FOMO – fear of missing out. They want to be there, they want to see it, they're very connected to technology. Do they know the latest sports results? Are they going to be able to talk about it during the coffee break, during the lunch, when they meet their friends?*

Do they know the latest fashion? What's on at the movies? Busy, busy, busy, busy, busy. "Oh, my gosh," they say when someone gives them a bit of news. "I didn't know that." That's why people love gossip so much. "Oooh, somebody knows something that I don't." Instant hit.

And all the while, with the busyness they are disconnecting with themselves, so if they truly want to manifest, live the life that they desire, then the universe, the multiverse, the eighth dimensions of creativity, well, it is waiting for them to put their order on the tray instantly, just like a McDonald's hamburger.

But we need to ask, what is it that they desire? What is it that they truly believe they deserve? For many feel they are not deserving of it. If you feel undeserving then it will not manifest. Why do so many people who win what you term the lotto, you know that game where all the money comes in, they often lose it very quickly. Only a few retain it and make it to be something more.

For they don't deem themselves worthy.

But we would like them to get what you term a right royal slapping. C'mon, wake up, wake up, wake up! Look at yourselves in the mirror, the beautiful perfection that you are.

All That Is has sent you here for this adventure, which is just one of your lifetimes. What is it that you desire? Start creating it. Start being joyful. Start celebrating. Don't wait for the perfect woman or for the perfect man to come and rescue you. Nobody's coming to rescue you. You are rescuing yourself. What is there to rescue? You chose this position. You chose this experience. No blame. Love yourself. As you begin to love yourself, that love is going to emanate and vibrate, and you will now attract another on your bandwidth.

If you wish to start receiving, what is it that you are giving?

For it is aligned with your emotions, your colour and your vibration. See how animated this one is now saying these words? For this one has learnt to give now to herself, for she sees what happens when she doesn't give to herself, when she doesn't accept herself.

We told her in this session, and the other session, that we won't let her down, and she was a little bit disturbed before she went to bed last night and she thought, "No, I have to connect with my guides, and I've got to write down what it is we wish to talk about today." Her mind was blank and her connection wasn't great, because she was tired. She did three sessions yesterday; she was pushing herself wanting to please others, instead of wanting to take a break and taking a walk.

We let her ramble on. We knew it was a whole lot of nonsense, but we knew she needed to get out onto the paper in order for her to go to sleep. So, this morning, we let her know that last night was nonsense. She felt the urge to sit down and quickly connect with us. As soon as she did that, she was fresh, she was in alignment and those words came out rapid-fire. Boom, boom, boom, boom, boom. There was no doubt. Has she not delivered today, Alba?

A: Yes, she's delivered.

J: *For these words are our words coming through her. Our mouthpiece for humanity. We want humanity to take a stand at this time. These are hard times, but these are soldiers of the light. These are our light army. She is our Commander in Chief, you are our General, Alba. We are broadcasting for everybody to take a stand for themselves, be steady in self. Know that the turbulence will come, but it will not suck you up and spit you out.*

You will go where it has been planned. You are situated on this Earth plane now as beacons, either holding the tone or playing the tune with others, connecting with others. This is an exciting time of your Earth's evolution. The revolution for the evolution of yourself is within. Drop the expectations. Bring in the joy and the celebration. Look at the ones in your lives whom you love. Love them.

Reach out. Lift those brothers and sisters who are lower and feeling depressed, and then as you do that to them, those will then come back to you when you are feeling lowered.

This is a time for a glorious chain to be built, for there is a chain of events that are unfolding as we speak.

There is much happening in the multiverses for the ascension, for the times are coming when all will hear the trumpets and, please, no consternation for the nations.

For this will bring all nations together in alignment where there has been fragments, and where there has been war.

The golden era will soon be amongst you all.

Connect with the eighth, cut away fourth. Three, two, one. Let's have

LIFT-OFF!

It is time for lift-off, Alba.

A: Wonderful, thank you so much. Who have we been talking with today?

J: *Simon Peter and James, orchestrated by Urka, with archangel Uriel's light coming through the middle, to spread the message.*

A: Wow, that's quite a celebration. Thank you so much for that. What do we call this session today?

J: *Ascension.*

A: Is there anything else, or do you feel we are complete?

J: *Alba, this one is most excited, for you only have two sessions left.*

A: Yes.

J: *She wants the book to go out, she wants the audio to be heard. She wants the messages to be spread, she wants the borders to be open.*

But we say as a collective, coming to you from the eighth of creation "open up your borders within", for how many of you have your borders that are closed?

Closing you off to the life that you should be celebrating, and joyfully living today. If you have problems with emotions, get hold of the feelings counsel. Reach out to those loved ones.

Alba, we thank you from the collective of the 4046 for the work that you have done for the navigation for today's script.

A: Thank you so much for that. I know that my guides are with me too, and I'm sure that they are working together.

J: *They are joyfully celebrating.*

A: Thank you.

CHAPTER ELEVEN (Session 425)

PREPARATION FOR ASCENSION

In this hypnosis session we continue the discourse as Jill visits a tuning tower where each planet is seen as a different vibration. The guide speaks about Saturn and its inhabitants, the Fibonacci code, and provides details about the great leveller and how to prepare ourselves for Earth's ascension.

J: *I was escorted up some stairs that were made of glass, and Earth was just a tiny dot far, far, far away. The stairs were lit up like glass crystal, and there were lights on either side showing me up the stairs. On the sides were squadrons of space ships, all in triangles like a pyramid shape, just flying in and out, hovering around, sort of doing a fly-by.*

A: Yes.

J: *I then looked down at my body and I was very, very tall, with a soft white robe and long grey hair and a long grey beard. Sort of like Gandalf or a wizard. I was holding a staff, the rod, they call it the rod, that you see in Egypt, in my right hand.*

A: What is this? What does it look like? What does this rod look like?

J: *It looks similar to what you would term a shepherd's crook. So, in the old days, the shepherds had a walking stick with a soft curve at the top.*

A: Yes. What else did you see?

J: *Well, I sense that I'm on my way to the tuning tower.*

A: Tell me more about this place. What does it look like?

J: *It's similar to a castle, but a skinny one and it is made of crystal, the stairs are similar to a grand staircase, sweeping up high into the turret. As you walk over the stairs, it looks like it's a piano. Coloured lights and all different vibrations come out of it, just like a tune, it is as if you're greeted with a melody. So, I then walked towards the top of the turret. At the top of the turret, it's just like being inside a spaceship because we have a viewing platform of all the planets. I've got what looks like an armchair that you can sit on, it turns into any direction of the entire turret, right around.*

A: Yes.

J: *When I swing around on the armchair, I have a console in front of me, the entire circle is a console. Each viewing platform is a large window that I can look through. I can tune into any of the planets, and each planet has its own vibration and its own colour. I'm in charge of holding the vibrations in place for each planet. I am making sure that the star-seeded lineage from each planet has the correct tone, meaning the correct hue, the correct vibration, the correct frequency for the energetic form that takes place on each of those planes, for they are planes, they are then plan-et, planets.*

A: Which one are you focused on right now?

J: *Saturn. It is this one's home base in another fractal.*

A: What's happening on Saturn?

J: *There's a lot of creativity going on here, there are a lot of artists here, a lot of musicians. It's a time to sit back and think about what steps one would like to take next. It is very contemplative, there is no time restriction, it's like being on a holiday, but working at the same time. So, the energy that flows through the beings that used to come here are very soft, very gentle, but highly creative.*

A: Do those energies on Saturn have a physical form?

J: *Some choose to have physical form; others look like what you term ghosts.*

A: Those that choose a physical form, is it like a human-type form?

J: *Yes.*

A: Do they look similar to the ones on Earth, or do they look different?

J: *No, they choose a very similar form, and they choose a form which they deem to be what is perfection in their eyes, of what they think their best attributes are. So, if they are into noses, they would have and choose what's deemed the perfect nose, or the perfect hands. That's how they create; they finely tune themselves, tune their beings. When they're comfortable with their appearance, then they settle back and start creating.*

A: How do they create their forms in Saturn? Is it similar to how we do it on Earth?

J: *There's a crystalline bed, and they glide into position, their thought forms start melding and moulding around the visual perception of what it is they wish to achieve. The different crystalline structures are put in place for them, for the energy that they need to absorb in each area.*

A: That seems almost similar to the etheric body of a human on Earth.

J: *Yes, but this is why they're choosing that human form, and that is why, did we not say, that you are crystalline of nature?*

A: Yes.

J: *That is why we can communicate with you, for crystal is a conductor, and that is why we repeatedly say, clean up your act, take out all the dross, remove what weighs you down so that you can be a finely-tuned machine. When we talk machine, we're not taking away the human side of things, but meaning operating at your full potential, for most of you are sluggish, and there are so many humans that wish to learn communication. They say, "We can't communicate with our guides, how is it that this one and that one has such clear communication?" Because they have cleaned up their crystalline structure, and in the process of cleaning it, the cleaner it gets then the more information you are able to absorb.*

A: When Jill saw herself going up into this tuning tower, what is happening to the Earth now? Why did she need to see that? Is there something that is being re-tuned or tuned up?

J: *Yes, as this one tunes the planets and holds their vibrations in place, did we not say in a previous session that it's time for the Earth, for Gaia, to take her place back in her lineage?*

Her vibrations are rising, they're getting lighter and lighter. She too is clearing up her act, for there is much that is weighing her down. The humans that she has been host to have poisoned her rivers and her skies. Her breathing is not at the potential that it should be, and as humans have not reached their full potential, the humans are now dragging the host down.

She no longer wishes to be dragged down, and that is why we showed this one the root system of Gaia, and it is when you do your work, Alba, by cutting the ties with the golden scissors, and so it is time for Gaia to cut her roots to this particular area in the solar system, so she to can ascend and rise above.

Now, the humans that wish to rise with her need to be crystalline, they need to be light as well, but this is free will. How do they hear the call of the trumpet? The quickening of the tempo? The frequencies that are rising? Do they not hear them? Do they not see the signs of agitation everywhere as people wish to break free, just like Gaia?

A: So, what happens when Gaia breaks free of these vibrations? What do the humans feel?

J: *The humans will feel the trembling, for there will be many Earth shifts and Earth changes. For if you strap yourself into a jumbo jet seat to fly to another country, as that jet takes off, do you not feel it? They do not serve the drinks while the plane is taking off, do they?*

A: No.

J: *Yes, because there would be a mess everywhere. So, there will be turbulence. We have spoken of this before. You know, Alba, this one replied to one of the questions asked yesterday by the previous session, and the lady couldn't understand the wording that we were using. So, we are now going to be very precise in our communication that this transmission is reaching. She wanted to know what she had to prepare for. Just tell her and then she'll be okay. So, now we are going to detail it.*

A: Thank you.

J: *If you are listening to this transmission, and you have a problem with a family member, please to address this problem. Speak to them with an open heart. Do not go in wanting to be the winner, for a winner in our eyes is the one that does not have to get the last word. You do not need to have the response from that family member that you desire in order for you to elevate and rise above the situation. It is enough that you made peace with that energetic being. This way you set yourself free, you removed the roots, you cut the cords that's with the family members.*

Then we wish you to do the same with work colleagues, with friendships, all relationships. It is a time for communication, to be clear. No manipulation, just from your heart. You will be most surprised at how much turbulence you will be removing from your beings. Your energy will lift, you will have a spring in your step, and this is ascension, for you are rising above. So, that's relationships.

Then we hark on the same subject again, of physical things. This one had a discussion with the feelings council yesterday, as they set up their structure. We planted an idea into her head about emotions, and emotional beings, of which this planet is. when someone does not feel filled, when their heart and their essence and their core is missing something, that then is when they fill themselves up with things.

Sorry, Alba, this one needs to cough – she didn't have enough water this morning.

So, when these humans buy more things and more things, they are filling up the emotion, the void within. Now they look around them and see how they've progressed in their lives. Some of them don't need these things any more, for they are now learning who they are. So, it is now a time for giving away those old things, for you are no longer that old being. And as Alba came back from Peru, and had the need to paint her apartment, and freshen it up and change the décor, she was erasing the old energy that she no longer was.

All your things that you are holding onto are actually holding the old vibrations of "not enough." So why would you still have them there? For although you are not using them, the vibrations are holding you down. So, now is the time to get rid of them and declutter.

We want you to pick up an item and feel it, feel what it makes you feel like inside, what does it feel like in your heart. Pick up a book and place it on your heart, does this resonate? Meaning does this vibrate with me? Is it aligned? That's what resonate means. Is it in alignment? If the answer is no, if it does not, then it is time to gift this to somebody else. Does this jersey, jumper, pants, shirt, shoes, rings, whatever it is, do these paintings, do these carpets, rugs and this bedspread, do they resonate with me? When you pass them over to another, you will once again be lightened, for you are no longer holding on to that old energy.

Alba, you spoke with this one yesterday about not giving your power away, did you not?

A: Yes.

J: ***Well, when you give things away, you are reclaiming your power, for you are saying "I know now that I'm worthy, I know now that I'm good enough, I do not need to fill myself up with things anymore." In actual fact, the more you give away, the more you self-generate. So, Alba, relationships and things, and then what else do we have?***

What else do we have to get in order?

This energy form, (Jill sweeps her right hand from her forehead down) *that you chose to come and experience this particular adventure with, how are you honouring it? For as you honour this form,* (your body) *so it honours you. We wish for you to connect with each body part. Is it in a good condition? If it is not in a good condition, ask it what it needs, what it requires. You have acupuncturists, you have healers, you have massage therapists, you have nutritionists, kinesiologists and you have natural doctors.*

So, there are many ways that you can look after your form and the lungs which hold your breath. There is no life if there is no breath. It would really appreciate getting exercised in fresh air. Your skin being your largest organ, the pituitary and also your eyes, they would also love to have sunshine. Remove the sunglasses, and absorb some of the natural light.

When you've looked after your form, when you have looked after your relationship and you've decluttered all your things, what is then left but your thoughts? How do your thoughts serve you at this very moment? Are they heavy thoughts? Or are they light? Do you currently own and hold the thoughts that will allow you to rise with Gaia? That is why we say rise above situations and things. Your thoughts have to be light, not only about yourself, your behaviour, your actions, your reactions, your forms, but also about others.

When those thoughts are light, your mind will be quiet, and it will be open, like a flower when it rains, absorbing the moisture in order to grow. If it's tightly closed and it rains, it doesn't have the same capacity for joy. Does that answer your questions, Alba?

A: Yes, thank you. I do have a question about relationships, though. There are times when you have had issues with someone who's no longer around. Perhaps they've moved away, but it's been left with a strange sense in your gut and in your heart. Is there a way that we can make amends with those that we have issues with mentally and through meditation? In a way like that, where we can actually ask for forgiveness, or work things out in a different realm?

J: *You know, Alba, there are those on the Earth plane that are termed alcoholics.*

A: Yes.

J: *These alcoholics carry deep shame, and deep pain, and they drown their sorrows. When they drink, they initially feel high, but this does not last for long. Many drink because of emotional miscommunication, and the more they drink, the more they discolour their crystalline body – their form, their energy. When they lower the intake, and the body has time to regenerate, they will then be able to hold a communion with those that have passed over. That is one example.*

Another example is that you can sit down in a quiet place and have a dialogue, for none are separated, be it on this Earth plane or another, and we would once again like to give you the example of the orange and the segments. The one that has departed is one of the segments of the orange, and the other segment is that of one that is still on Earth, but they are held together by the pith, the matrix, the energetic cord, and so they are heard. For this one has been holding communion with her father who is no longer here. They had a tumultuous relationship where she was rejected and disowned for thirty years, it weighed heavily on this one for her self-worth. We have helped her through that, and she's learnt to sit in a quiet place and hold communion.

There are many Earthlings who have not made peace with themselves, for the words that were said or were not said with those that have now departed. But those that have departed know your thoughts, and know your heart, for they see things now with more clarity. They are able to get clarification on that human conversation, or human heartbeat. So, we would like to tell humanity that is listening, journal your feelings. Your loved ones will know what it is that you are writing. Speak to them in your hearts. They will hear you, for this is what it is to hold a discourse.

This is why we gave these twelve sessions the name The Discourse. Humans have to learn to communicate, communicate with each other, and to communicate with self. They need to start going within, stop cutting themselves off from their feelings, stop filling themselves up with food to make themselves and their heart feel full. Their heart is not feeling full with the more that they stuff inside their mouths. In actual fact, it is taxing their hearts.

They're not filling themselves up by buying things, they are not filling themselves up and making themselves feel better by denigrating another. This is all about communication, having and holding a discourse, a conversation with themselves, internally and externally.

Ascension is near; if they follow the steps that we have laid out as clearly and precisely and slowly as possible, then we are hopeful that you and this one no longer receive questions about what or how to prepare for the event, for the great leveller, for ascension?

For each human that wishes to ascend we ask, "What is it that you are doing in your current life, with your life? Do you think you are ready for ascension? Or do you have serious work to do?" Get on with it today!

A: Thank you for the preparation, but now the question is what is going to happen with this ascension? If we see Gaia breaking free, feeling the Earth jolting, what is it that we are going to feel? Is it going to be upheavals? Is it going to be hurricanes? Tornadoes? Floods? Or nothing at all? What is it that we are going to feel?

J: *Alba, all of the above.*

A: Okay.

J: *In the first session we spoke about this one and how you have different way-stations or landing platforms. You have your earthly incarnation and you live your life, you have an adventure. You came here to Earth in order to help yourself and help another. All of you have different missions. All of you are on this Earth plane as a piece of a puzzle. Take a few pieces out and the puzzle is not complete. Depending on the picture, one piece is not better than another, for without the piece, the picture is incomplete.*

So, where do they go to when the jolting, the shaking, the flooding, the earthquakes, and when the Earth breaks, where do they go? What happens to them? What happens to their energy?

What happens to their energetic form is the same that happens to them after any incarnation. They go to their landing platforms. A lot of them have a rest, greeted by their loved ones or their guides before the wise council evaluating how they do, how they did, what it is they wish to do. Go back with their soul family, one particular group, a cluster, a cluster within a cluster, different realms. You, like this one, has hypnotised many, do they not have all different deaths, Alba?

A: Yes.

J: *Yet they are on the other side of your Zoom, or on your couch in this current incarnation. It is a cycle. They are wishing to prepare for the, what you humans term, the unknown. This is what is causing consternation, and yet they might step out of their door and get killed in a car accident, or they might visit a doctor and find out they have cancer. They might have a brain tumour; they might fall off a building. There are many different ways to exit this human form.*

Do they get warned about those other deaths or ways of dying? No, many do not. So why would this be any different? They chose to come here at this time, for they are very important pieces of the puzzle for the lifting of the planet, for the golden era to be brought in.

Many humans are going to what you term pass away, and many humans are going to remain, for it is the particular mission that each individual being chose to experience. We do not wish for consternation, and that is why we told you in detail how best to prepare. For when one has prepared and followed all the steps mentioned just now, one has nothing to fear, for all are on a path.

A: Thank you. Can you tell me why you wrote or gave Jill the question or the statement, "The book of judgement is a reflection of your choices"?

J: *The book of judgement, and what is the book of judgement? What is one judging, who is one judging? For one thinks, that when one leaves this Earth plane, there will be others that are placing judgement on you. But the book of judgement is your life, it is the book of life. We say, we would like to call it the Book of Observation. For is observation not a better word? For humanity has a heavy heart when they hear the word judgement – to judge another or to judge self. We would like this to be replaced with The Book of Observing, and the Book of Observation.*

So, how is one observing oneself in one's life? If one had to give oneself a mark out of ten for how one is looking after one's energetic form, that one was gifted with. It is like a barometer.

Could they perhaps say "I could do better here, mmm, I'm a little bit slack in this particular area." It then takes the heaviness of the judgement away but rather an observation, as one ascends, one needs to observe oneself less, and enjoy the moments more. We do not wish for judging, for humans are what you term Olympic gold medallists when it comes to judgement.

They judge themselves because they feel others have more than them, more things, more beauty, better relationships, bigger homes, better careers. They then feel a lack, and then they start filling themselves up, and yet the more they fill the emptier they feel.

Alba, life on this Earth plane now offers so much beauty that is free for all. Why is humanity not taking their lungs and their legs out onto this planet to explore it and give gratitude? Gratitude and judgment, it is time you start having an attitude of gratitude, and a gratitude journal. Please to start journaling what it is that you have, the judgement will fall away.

For if money solved everything in this world, why then are those that you term rich committing suicide, getting divorced, and being treated for depression?

Humanity rather needs to look at that, to realise that the richness of life and living is not in monetary value, but in the very simple ways of life. Having a cup of tea with a good friend, reading a book, welcoming a new baby into the family, having dinner with family and friends, going for a walk, flying a kite, blowing bubbles, looking at a flower, enjoying the shade of a large tree under a hot summer's sun. Simple things, Alba. So many are blessed, and yet they want to panic and worry about ascension when they're not even connecting in the living moments that they have now.

A: Thank you for that. Two of the questions or statements that you gave us today are about codes. A codal index of the universe, and the Fibonacci code. Can you address these codes and what they mean?

J: *The Fibonacci is a sequence and a pattern that lies within all creation, making systems run smoothly, and it is mathematical perfection. Each form holds the code, the God Code, the Fibonacci code, the code of creation, the code of perfection. The universe has a codal index.*

This index holds the Fibonacci codes and other codes that you have yet to learn and experience, for there are many, many adventures that await you all. This Earth plane is on a depleted power generator, for although you have much beauty, it is going at a low frequency.

The codal index that is held by the All That Is, is a list of all the universes, all the multiverses, all the frequencies. Alba, you have a question there that you were going to ask this one, and it would be good to bring it in at this stage, about astrology and astronomy.

A: Yes, what is that? You got Jill to write down "I'm an astronomer of astrology."

J: *She was having a dream. We woke her up because we wanted her to discuss these words today so people can better understand themselves, for they are so enmeshed and entrenched in their*

3D human form, that they think that that is actually what they are, when in fact that is only an experience of what they are.

This one in the turret, the fractal of Jill in the crystalline turret, with all the frequencies, has a fine tuner and we showed her in the shower, just before you started this session today, of the images of colours of astronomy, of all the planets, holding their vibrations, which are frequencies, energy which are forms, colour and light.

Humans listening to this particular transmission need to buy your book The Discourse, *for in the first two sessions that are written in the book, that will not be transmitted through the airwaves gives a detailed description of life and creation being formed, the photonic structure.*

Each human comes from a lineage. They look up their DNA or their ancestral lineage at a website on this Earth plane which is actually not their lineage, but which is rather just an experience currently in the particular time-space continuum. The planets that they come from vibrate at a certain frequency and colour wave, and this one, being the astrologer, studies and harmonises the frequencies.

She sees the colours, she knows which ones blend well, and so there was a choosing from all the planets to bring out the star seeds in a harmonic convergence, working together, blending together, coming to the Earth, working with Gaia, with the frequencies that they hold. Astrology, astrological signs of how those planets are aligned with the sun and the moon and the turning and the frequency, so the seed is planted inside the mother, and it germinates and the human form comes out. That human form resonates, filling the vibrations like a recipe while they are growing. They then come out under a particular sign.

The music, the celestial music of the spheres. Those vibrations come through the mother into the womb, into the baby, and that particular baby, as it grows, will resonate with particular frequencies and sounds that others are not aligned with. For it is their particular frequency, under their sign, the way the planets were aligned, the sound and the vibrations that were generated through time-space continuum into their energetic form that makes them who they are, experiencing those frequencies.

That is why you have some Earthlings that will go to a rock concert and others to a classical soiree. For one's aligned to the classics, and another is aligned to the rock. But depending on the astrology from the astronomy, there may be a blending where they can listen to the classic and the rock, but some always gravitate to a particular sound which gives them great joy. For, Alba, if you listen to a particular song, it gives you a certain feeling does it not?

A: Yes.

J: *It means you are aligning with your vibrational lineage. It is neither wrong, it is neither right, it is just what works for that particular alignment.*

A: I have a question about that because recently I asked my guides about my work. It's been a long time since I had a dialogue with them, and I was told that my voice was what people would recognise in the soul group, or in the alignment of those that I was working with. Can you tell me a little bit about that? Because I know my voice is unique, and it generates a certain vibration. How does my voice affect some people? I know it's like fingernails on a chalkboard to some.

(Both Jill and Alba laugh.)

J: *Wooh, judgy, judgy, Alba. Well, your voice it is your song, it is your melody, it is your alignment which is carried through. It is your frequency, your frequency is your ID, it aligns with the All That Is.*

Your frequency changes energetic form depending on which planet you decide to go to.

Depending whether you would like to be a comet, a human or any other form, what is it that you wish? But your ID, the identification of who you are, your code, your God Code, your God Code is encoded in you as an Alba, also when you were a Sasquatch, as it is in the blue avian fractal of you. This is important to understand that whatever form you take; it is your signature. Therefore, those who have had a parallel life with yours, they will then recognise your signature because they recognise your sound, your vibration, which is your frequency.

A: Wonderful, thank you. You also mentioned "association of weekly digestion." What do you mean by that? Why did you get Jill to write that down for us to discuss?

J: *Well, how do humans digest, and what does digestion mean? Are there not some that hold a conversation, and then the one says to the other, "Mmm, give me some time, I need to digest that." They need time to assimilate it, for they have learnt they do not have to be reactive. They do not have to give anybody any answer this red-hot minute because the other needs that information, or needs to know.*

No one controls you; you control yourself. You do not allow another to control and hand your power over to them and feel depleted.

So, then you need time to digest the words, and this is the biggest problem with humanity – they are reactive. They think they have to give an immediate response to any situation. Just look at drivers behind the wheel in a traffic jam. Immediately their instant reaction is to put their hand on the hooter at full blast, and they put their hands out the window, and they do little signs with their fingers do they not?

A: Yes.

J: *This is what we term reactive, had they thought about it, should they have had the time to digest the situation, they would realise that perhaps there was an accident ahead, or that a traffic light had broken down. Many different scenarios. By gesticulating, or adding their noise to it, is not helping the situation. In actual fact, it's agitating them more, as well as those around them. So, it's a weekly digestion, and what we mean by association is who do you associate with on a weekly basis? What have you done for that particular week? Perhaps you can set aside some time on a Sunday evening, before your new week starts, for many have meetings set in place, many have children that need to go to particular activities.*

Take time once a week to have a meeting with yourself, and digest not only how you've tracked over the last week, but also what you are about to encounter into your next week. Do not be reactive, learn to be what Alba says – the calm in the eye of the storm. This is a very good way to know how you are preparing for ascension.

For when one reacts one always hands one's power to another.

This is the time for holding one's power in a gentle way in self, in self-communion, in holy communion. That's why we said on a Sunday, to do this on a Sunday, for this is generally a day of rest for the humans when not much is expected from them. This vessel, your form, your energy, your God Code, it is a holy vessel.

When you hold a communion with yourself it is holy, it is time to bless yourself for doing everything that self has done to this point. When you do bless self and thank self, then you are giving holy communal thanks, to the All That Is, for this life, for this current adventure. Before this life terminates, one needs to think about what one has been given. What is one grateful for? What an incredible adventure that one has had, and as one gives gratitude, one reaches the point of ascension quicker and quicker. For as one gives gratitude, one opens the doors to infinite new possibilities.

A: Wonderful. Thank you so much. Is there anything else, or do we feel that we've completed today's discourse?

J: *Alba, we think this is a very important discourse today. We do not think that there would be anybody listening to this transmission that have now not heard our trumpet trumpeting. For she is our messenger. She is a messenger from source, to all source's children, for source wishes to expand and as source expands, so do you all.*

What is it that you choose to experience and put into your storybook called your life? Your book of judgements or observations. We wish all who once they have finished listening to this transmission to look into themselves, to look and see where their adjustments need to be made, where the peace-making needs to occur. Where decluttering is required, and spend time with self and honour the body, this piece of cloth, your meat suit that clothes the energetic field, it does so that you can experience all that you can be. Go out and experience and expand, find the joy, live in the moment.

So be it.

A: Thank you, thank you very much for that. Who are we speaking with today?

J: *Urka.*

A: Urka. Thank you very much, Urka. What do we call this session today?

J: *Preparation for Ascension.*

A: Wonderful. That will be an eye-opener for people, very good.

J: *We need to grab attention, Alba, for many are slumbering,*

A: Yes. Thank you for opening ears today. Hopefully, they'll do their homework. With that, I'd like you to go ahead and disconnect from Jill. Jill I'd like you to go ahead and retrieve all your energy.

CHAPTER TWELVE (Session 428)

LIGHT-WORKERS UNITE

In this hypnosis session we finish the discourse. Jill visits the Hall of Judgement, where there is a large meeting of intergalactic delegates to discuss the plan about the great leveller on Earth. We discuss the light that will bring in the true age of enlightenment, the lightworkers, and the importance of living in the moment of now.

A: What do you sense?

J: *The Halls of Judgement.*

A: Tell me about that.

J: *As I was rising above the water, I was greeted by the blue being I saw yesterday. It was Jesus, and he has blue light all around him. Now he's taking me into the Halls of Judgement. There are so many rooms here, so much discussion going on, big, big tables, lots and lots of books. There's a lot of coming and going. It's like what you would imagine the United Nations to be like, lots of dignitaries arriving.*

A: What do they look like, these dignitaries?

J: *Like something out of* Star Wars.

A: Can you describe some for me?

J: *Well, one's just come past me. They've got a very, very big... how do I even describe the head? It's like a wasp, so it's got a very, very big, bulbous head, the back of the head is round, and then coming longer and longer in the front and then tiny little ears, and it has eyes that come out on stalks, stalks so the eye can move up and down, backwards and forwards. Its neck is like a vertebra, if you had to have a human vertebra, you know, the bones without the flesh, well the neck is like that, like lots of little vertebra put together, and it's all black, black vertebra. The head's all grey and you can see its veins under the skin. It's almost translucent, it's a very different looking creature.*

A: How tall is it?

J: *Very tall.*

A: And what about the rest of the body? Is it a humanoid body or an insectoid body?

J: *No, it's insectoid, it's insectoid, yeah.*

A: Are they dressed in any way or do they just have an insectoid body?

J: *This one's got a cloak on it. It is covered right down to the ground, and it seems to float rather than walk. And then, to my right in the passage, I can see some… they call them the Nordics. These are very blond, very pale skin, beautiful eyes, and they are just going to where they need to go; they're going to a meeting in the Great Temple.*

A: What do you look like? Look down at your body.

J: *I'm… I look… that's weird. I look like I'm made out of stone.*

A: Tell me more about that.

J: *If you got a really big rock and you dropped it, and it shattered into a thousand pieces then you glued it together, well, that's what my body looks like.*

A: Does it have a humanoid shape or is it all over the place?

J: *Yeah, like the Incredible Hulk, that kind of a shape but very soft flowing eyes. I can cry tears, so I've got emotion, but I can shape into different forms. It depends what I want to project. Today, I'm here as strength, strength for the galaxy. That's why I'm showing the stone. I'm set in stone for my people, so they won't be able to budge me.*

A: What or who are your people?

J: *Earth.*

A: Tell me more about this meeting you're going to. This Hall of Judgement that you speak of, what does it look like?

J: *She's seen it many times in her dreams when she thinks of the Halls of Learning. Many beings go to similar buildings when they pass over for their lessons. It has many steps, grand steps leading up to the entrance. It also has big, big, big, big pillars of light, and then a deep recess, but it's a very solid structure like marble, and each room has a crystalline chamber, and there's different lights in different rooms, depending on what energy you wish to transmute in a particular meeting, so if there's agitation from a particular galaxy, and that particular embassy arrives with those agitated ambassadors, we need them to be calmed down, so then there's a particular hue that we use that then calms them.*

A: Where is this building, is it in a different dimension or is it in a physical place?

J: *It's in a physical place. It's a central point where you come to through your hyperspace, through your wormholes. They come in through the wormhole from all the different galaxies, so it's a meeting place that is central for all.*

A: And when we started, you called it The Hall of Justice or…

J: *The Hall of Justice and The Halls of Judgement.*

A: So, why are we here today? What is this meeting all about?

J: *I'm coming here to represent Earth and all the star-seeded lineage. I've called in the counsellors from all the different galaxies to find out how the plan's going, for there's great agitation on Earth.* (Jill cries.)

A: Yes, there is.

J: *There is much suffering. I need to know if the plan is running smoothly. I need to know that the galactic soldiers are in place, that the ships are ready, that the landing platforms are smooth, that the way-stations have their welcoming committees, and that the counsellors are instructing the light army that are on Earth, through their portals, through their rays of colour, that they're receiving the transmissions correctly at this given time.*

For it's like a family tree, Alba. It trickles all the way down, all the different platforms. There's much alignment that needs to take place. For as this one was putting the Feelings Counsel into place on your planet as a small example, as she put up 4 I Am Universe as a Facebook page, as we arranged the Peru trip through Antonio to get the family back together again, as we aligned you with this one, as we aligned Tabaash with you and all your teachings, Alba, in all your channels, and the group of the Essenes coming together again, and the different energies that are distributed throughout your Earth plane, your different pockets of colour, your bandwidth.

As you can see there is much that needs to be aligned. There are those that are contracted through their star-seeded lineage from the various galaxies in the planet systems, that came for a particular mission, and they have a use-by date. This one had a conversation with you just before you started this morning and she said, "I will go when I'm done." When she's come to do what it is that she's come to do, then it will be her use-by date, as it is with all Earthlings that had been here from time immemorial.

Everybody has a use-by date, and yet they fear the unknown.

So, today, my job is to show strength in the chamber for the Earthlings, for my star-seeded lineage, for I have been on all the galaxies, and all the colour rays, and that is why I have the light that holds them all in place.

That is why they chose Jill. They chose her for her strength, for she holds all the colour ways, for all the fractals, and all the factions.

I'm at the council today to make sure that there are what you term no glitches. Everything is in place. The energy is on its way. There will be great upliftment.

Although many will be unsettled, there will be a great settling and a great rejoicing, for they will have accomplished their missions.

A: Will they know that they've accomplished their missions when it happens?

J: *There will be no doubt. This one is now being shown the end of the Second World War, with all the avenues and all the streets with the people cheering, and the flags fluttering. It will be so. Did they not know that the war is over?*

A: Yes.

J: *It was a great rejoicing, and so it shall be again, for this has been the great duality. This has played out for a very long time. You know, Alba, when we take you to the Egyptian times, which was the true age of enlightenment, we ask, what has happened between that time and this time?*

Many Earth years have passed, and what happened to the knowledge? Why was the knowledge suppressed? But those Egyptians, those powerful ones live amongst you now, with that knowledge, with that light, with that great power, and so many will be empowered once again, to remember who they are.

They are beings of great light, yet they weigh themselves down with human worries. This is not a time for worry, this is a time to get to work, to clear your minds and to clear your cupboards.

We speak and we speak and we speak yet you hear us not.

What more is it that we need to say? You are crystalline of

structure. What you are as an Earthling is your overcoat. Take your overcoat off to remember who you are, fear not. This has been predicted for aeons. It is time, it is the time of the crossing, it is time to cross over, it is time to let the light in. That is why we termed it The Golden Era. You have been yoked and enslaved for hundreds of years, but now is the time for the yoke to be removed, but nobody can do it for you, you have to do the removing.

This one was recently working with a young man, trying to uplift him and show him a different way. She said to him, "You've got a hammer and a nail, and you have put the nail in your own foot and you've hammered it in securely. Now you're running around and around in circles, saying, "I can't go anywhere, I can't go anywhere" and blaming everyone else, and not looking at yourself.

Yet you were the one who put the nail in your own foot, and because you put it in your own foot, you can remove it, you can move freely. And so, we say once again that these humans who have enslaved themselves through the programming and have the yoke around their necks, the burden on their shoulders, through the programming, they can break the programming, but it is deeply embedded in their systems, in their psyches. What will they do then? What will they do if they turn off the blue box? Then they have to look at each other for entertainment and conversation. And what is it that they will converse about? Will they continue to converse about the exterior?

At what stage, and at what age, will they be when they start talking and discussing about the interior, for it is the interior who they truly are. The exterior is just a vehicle to express themselves, the body is not who they are. They are energy, they are a God Code, a particle of light in the All That Is.

But this exterior cloak or coat called your human body, it gets paid so much attention, so much money is spent on it, for you listen to the marketers. But what is spent on the internal? On the thought process? On feeding one's soul? One's light body? Do you rather busy yourself with people and doing things, instead of knowing yourself?

This is what those who say they are afraid really need to look at, for we say they are spending too much on the exterior. If they knew their interior, they would not be asking the questions, and they would not be holding fear. A human's fear is a barometer of what they need to now pay attention to.

A: Very good. I'd like to get back to the plan because as you're going into that meeting you say everything is getting prepared. Who came up with this plan first of all?

J: *The Commander in Chief and the Council of Archangels.*

A: What was happening that they needed to do this? Is there anybody else?

J: *Also, the disciples, they are there, they are the fractals of the Archangels, and the son of God. For it is time for his return, and yet humans will deem this to be in a physical presence, yet he is sending his light from deep within the galaxy to humanity.*

We said this is a light, an energy, that these humans have never experienced before. All will receive it equally, and so it will be a great leveller. For when this energy hits this planet, this Earth plane, all will have eyes that can see.

The scales will fall away, and the light will intermingle with their energetic beings. They will radiate Christ-like light. There will be many changes, for when one sees differently, one cannot but change.

You had a human that said if you keep looking at things the same way, things will never change. Change the way you look at something, and then you will have change. Alba, we want to now look at matter and the field.

When we speak about the field, we speak about the energy that is there for you all, a field of energy. The photons and the photonic structures and the light, the frequency, the vibration, and the colour. Humans often have a feeling of lack, when they want to have a feeling of abundance, and they say, "Give it to me and then I will believe, I will believe in you. Give it to me and then I will trust you, my guide, but I need it. I need the new car, I need to know where I'm going to live, I need to know who I'm going to marry. This is what I'm asking for. Give it to me, and then there will be trust, and we always flip it, because it is an emotion.

We say feel it, for you are the creators. You were created in order to create, so what is it that you are creating? What is it that you are feeling?

What is it that you wish to create? Because it is not the matter that makes the field, it is the field that creates the matter. So, what is it that matters to you, to the listeners that are listening to this transmission? What really matters that you need to create and make it into matter? Be careful what it is that you wish for, for we in the field distribute equally. You had a human in your recent questions/answers on your platform stating not all are equal.

A: That's right.

J: *They are many still that do not understand the energy, the form, the contracts, the wishes, the desires, the expansion, and the contraction. All are equal, all are given free will to choose their environments, their earthly adventures, and all their other adventures.*

So, if one chooses a particular lifestyle without an arm, poverty-stricken, and yet another is a professor living in what you term an exquisite abode, and then the third person looks at them both and says, "There's the professor in his exquisite abode, and here is this poor beggar in India, with an arm missing, and in dire poverty." It is impossible to see them as equal, we do not see them as equal, and yet perhaps in a parallel life the beggar is the professor, and the professor is the beggar.

So, there is much for humanity to learn, but the great leveller will change people's perceptions. Much will rise to the surface. There will be the largest discourse in living history. Many voices will be heard, there will be a what is termed a babbling, a babbling in the streets. It is time for people to remember their voice boxes. It is time for their portals of light to express what resides within.

It is a time for feeling, creating, energising, upliftment, and rising above the situations that they have created, that they have chosen to experience, in order for expansion to take place, for they are the cell, the tiny little organism in the All That Is, made in the image of God.

So, if they are that pulse of light that comes from source, some will be a short pulse, others will be a longer pulse, and yet where will they go? They go back to the All That Is, all the different landing platforms, all the different way-stations, all the different experiences, different light, different vibrations, different energetic forms, different formats.

There is much to look forward to. Please, this is a time for knowing oneself, therefore we say, why clutter yourselves with the nonsensical? When the light arrives, will you be ready to meet it, or will you be too full of clutter?

A: So, I have a question about that because sometimes I'm feeling that you're talking about one way will happen, and then I hear another way. With this great leveller are we going to stay here on Earth to experience this and rejoice? Or will we be beamed up to the platforms and the way-stations to rejoice there, does that make sense?

J: *Did we not say that the light-workers will be lifted in a nanosecond?*

A: Yes, so we're talking about the light-workers? Okay.

J: *Did we not say that all that are listening to this transmission are the light army? If they are not listening to this transmission, then they are listening to other transmissions, for all who are part of the plan will be instructed, receiving their guidance from the great Halls of Justice, through their interstellar lineage, their star-seeded lineage, their galaxies, their planets.*

Their brothers and their sisters are assisting them at this time. Many souls who have their light bodies in this 3D form before they return are killed in what you term car accidents or murdered, cancer, drownings, horse accidents, many, many, many different ways to evacuate this 3D body. Those who were not ready to evacuate for they had work to do, like this one, we brought her back through what you term a near-death experience, and she was able to rise out of the 3D overcoat and see herself in that bed.

And so, it is that you can rise above and then return to the 3D, through your Merkabah, through your alignment with the All That Is. There are many who fear death and so we hope that this transmission will settle many.

A: How do we know if our children are light-workers? Are there any signs to be aware of for those who have small children, or are concerned about them?

J: *How shall we answer this?*

Many of the children that have come in now are of what we term a higher – meaning lighter – light-infused vibrational energetic being than the older generation. Let's say, Alba, that your wattage, and this one's wattage, is growing a little dim, and they are the brighter bulbs.

They hold much light, for all those children that are coming in now, right up to their forties, are volunteers, specifically stepping forward with new abilities and a new way of looking at things. That is why you always get the younger generation to come in and stir things up, change things with their music, their new language, with the way they express themselves through their haircuts, their clothes, their terminology.

These young beings may be children, but they are ancient ones, specifically chosen for the ascension of Gaia. For this is a celebration in the galaxies, and they have sent their finest as honour students specifically for this mission. For this is a very important mission. This is what's termed a special occasion, for it is a graduation. It is a graduation of Gaia, so it is the honour students that are here to do the honourable work and to honour Gaia, for she has held on her body many, many millions of humans holding adventures. But, Alba, there are codes that have been laid on this Earth plane, waiting for activation to engage with the energy that is coming towards us, it is what we call fusonic, this one saw a bit of it yesterday.

A: Was that the blue being?

J: *We would like humanity to look up the term blue energy. Why we chose the blue. Blue is needed at this time, there are many fractals shades of blue. There are many blue beings on your Earth plane now. This is a very strong colour wave, energetic photonic, fusonic power.*

A: This blue being was very large, was it not? (Jill nods.) So, do we see these blue beings all around our planet? Is this what they are doing, are they activating?

J: *This blue light, this is the Christ light. When you think it's golden light or white light, it is blue light, and this blue light is what she saw at the start of the session when Christ was lifted up over the lake and she was lifted with Christ, for she saw him as she left the heavy body and rose above to look back at Wanaka. It was his light pulling her up, up to the Halls of Justice, leading the way.*

Are you not known as the blue planet?

A: Yes.

J: *Yes, and we have the shield, the energetic shield protecting the Earth, because of the power of the vibration of the blue, and the honeycomb bracing with our blue avatar beings, the bird beings, looking after the trap doors, looking after the portals, and that is why they are blue.*

A: This being that she saw, was it one of the bird beings? Or was it different, just the energy?

J: ***No, she was visited by Christ, Yeshua, Jesus. That is why this one felt the emotion.***

A: Okay, I understand, all right. So, we've got some information that you've given us. One thing that's very interesting is, today is the day, tomorrow is not here, yesterday has gone. Why have you written that for us today?

J: (Jill lets out a very big sigh.) *Humanity lives with a 24-hour time period, where they monitor their movements, not so? And so, we speak of yesterday, today, and tomorrow. Most of your listeners want to know about tomorrow, not so? Do you not have clairvoyants in great demand on this Earth plane? For everybody wants to know, they want to know their future, and yet you have many, many Earthlings holding onto the past. This yesterday, all the pain, all the sorrow, all the joy, all the experiences, that they have already had. So here they are talking about what was past, gone. Then, in front, you have the tomorrows group; who am I going to meet? Where am I going to live? What kind of job am I going to do? Should I do this? Should I do that? What's best for me?*

So, they divide themselves, in the past and in the future. But while they are doing that, what is happening in the present? For if they are spending their time on memories of the past and hopes for the future, who is attending to the present? So, we say you have the present because it has been pre-sent, and so it is presented to you as a gift, this moment in time.

You will never have this specific moment again.

You've had the past; your so-called future is not here yet. You have this moment. So, what are they doing with the moment? For if they spend this present moment creating, putting into the field, we say, hand it over to us we know what's in your hearts, but it is free will.

Unless you have trust in our guidance, create it, hand it over in this beautiful moment. Should the Earthlings do this, their next moments can be nothing but what they have created. So, if they are living in turmoil, what do they think will be the next moment? How are they addressing the current moment?

So, we keep on harping about the clutter. How does one create if there is a room full of clutter? How do you get a new room unless you take all the clutter away and then you can create the new space, be it the girl or the boy of your dreams, the perfect job, the gorgeous home, the new garden, the children, by living in the present moment? Uncluttered thoughts leave room for expansion and a lighter way of being.

A: Very good, thank you. What is the difference between the Intergalactic Federation of Light and the Galactic Federation of Light? Is there a difference?

J: *When we term the galactic, we term the singular, and when it is intergalactic it is the multiverses instead of the uni, the one verse. We woke this one up with the words galactic and intergalactic because we wanted to remind the audience today that they are not Earthlings.*

This is not who they are, this is what they are playing. These are the acts, the one-act, the two-acts, the three-acts play that they are playing on this Earth playground. But they are galactic beings from the multiverses. They are all different, they all have different strengths, or they come in their different colour waves, their different photonic structures, their different wavelengths, bandwidths, and they are a kaleidoscope of colours.

They give themselves names like black, white, Red Indians, Eskimos, Chinese, all the different colours, all the different skin tones, but we've told this one before why would any human judge another when they were once that themselves? Why would they judge themselves? For there are many selves. Do you see we say, "themselves" not "self?"

You choose many different incarnations. What if we said you were an insect creature? Oh, no. Oh, I'm not going to be the insect creature. I'm just going to be the Nordic because that is what's similar to what you are now. Familiarity. But you have been in many forms. If we had to show you the forms you have been, there would no longer be any judgement of another.

For this is what we term a cosmic joke, that humanoids are squabbling in the playground about the different colours that they are when if they had to really see their family lineage and their ancestry through the multiverses, their imagination cannot begin to envisage the shapes, the forms, the structures.

Alba, what if we told you that one being's head had an eye on the top, an eye on the front, an eye on the back, eyes on either side, pale pink, with blue ears? You would say, "Oooh, I wouldn't choose that form." What if we showed you a being with very, very long ears to the ground, like a basset hound, multi-coloured rainbow colouring, with a very, very, tall, thin face, and lots of polka dots all over the multi-colours and two big, round eyes, and long ears for hearing? This is a very colourful being, would you prefer this over the insectoid?

A: I don't know. I guess it depends where you are, right? If you want to be looking at your ceiling all the time with all those eyes, it would be an experience.

J: *We have to then say to you, what is form? You all chose the form that you are currently inhabiting. Does it suit you? What are you doing with your form? Are you honouring the form that you chose yourself? How are you looking after it? Are you nurturing it? Or have you rejected part of self, thinking yourself inadequate by looking at all those examples on the blue box as examples of what you should be?*

It is nothing but a marketing tool. We want you to look at your bodies. These bodies that came with you on your current adventure in order for you to express yourselves. It is time to look after them. But we see many changing the breasts, and the nose, and the lips, changing the hair colour, contouring of the cheeks.

Lots see imperfection when we see nothing but perfection, so why would one need to alter oneself in a different image when the All That Is gave you your image in its image, your photonic structure, perfectly tuned to this specific incarnation?

How much time do you spend unhappy with your image?

We gave this one an example of humanity, and we say there are those that are like a fish but they want to be a lion. Then we said, start exhibiting the characteristics of the lion to be big and brave, and strong and powerful. We wish humanity to be who they are, not a Jill, not an Alba, not a Dolores Cannon, not a Steve Dicks, not a Sylvia Peters, not a film star, or a YouTube sensation, none of those others, for they are all taken.

You who are listening, we want you to know that you are unique. There is no one like you in the entire multiverse. You came in your specific alignment from the planets, with your star-seeded lineage, through matter, dark matter, antimatter, through the point of creation, in a burst of energetic form, creating your bandwidth.

Why would you reject yourself and see nothing other than perfection? It is time to lift each other up, and that is why we brought in the fun-eral. It is time to have fun. These have been rough times. We wish for the energetic change, we wish all that are listening to this transmission to start creating anew, fresh and invigorating.

It's time to look at their form and say, I will no longer drag you around. I'm sorry, please forgive me, I love you. Then you will step into your light vehicle and be aligned with your Merkabah, which will take you wherever you choose.

Alba, this is truly going to be a time for enlightenment. This is exciting, this is invigorating, for it is uplifting and it is expansion. Why would one choose to contract oneself through another's words, through the blue box's programming? This is a time to remove the yoke and step into who you truly are. Everyone is in place. It is a great game. We said it is time for the party to begin, and what gifts will each listener give to the party, for how can they run and have fun and games if they are dragging themselves around?

A: Can you talk a little bit about the body, for all of those who are ill?

J: *What would you like to know, Alba?*

A: Well, you've talked about us honouring our body, and some of them, well many of them right now are under medical care, with all sorts of illnesses, diabetes, everything. What would you like to tell those people about their bodies? Is there a way for them to rejuvenate that body, change the body with thinking?

J: *Firstly, we would like them to know that they are loved. We are sending them our light, for many of them have lost their way. There's been a disconnect. They, too, have forgotten who or what they are, who they live for, and why they are alive.*

But, Alba, this does not cover all who are ill. There are many who are ill who have taken this on as an experience, not only for themselves but for those who they had an agreement with.

For the caregivers have learned much through the caring of those who have decided to carry an impairment, and there are others who have taken on an illness in order to exit the body, for there are many ways one exits this planet.

But for those who have not chosen the illness as an exit strategy, who can still be helped, it is through the change of the photonic structure, through vibration, colour, and thought. It is nothing other than vibration changing the photonic structure.

There are machines like yours that are able to go through the human body with a specific oscillation. For did we not many sessions ago show you the example of the metal steel with the sand on top, plugged into the electric output? Turn up the volume and the pattern changes. So it is with the patterns held within. They will get a mass or a darkness which contracts, so that area no longer flows, so it needs a new energy to come in.

Okay, so now we're giving this one an example that most listeners will be able to understand, of a cloud. If you lie on your back and look at the clouds, some of them look like a big cloud, and yet the wind comes along, which is energy, and it hits that cloud, and that mass that was so big slowly starts to dissipate until...where did it go? There is no longer a cloud, and yet the cloud was there. And so, it is within; the form changes. Do you not on your Earth plane have what you term energy healers? What is an energy healer, Alba?

A: Well, they use their intention and vibration and light, in their mind, anyway. They bring in, mmmm, let me see. They are a conduit.

J: *So, are some of these energy healers not absent healers, but from afar? How is that possible? Because whether a person is physically next to another person, using its energy, or is what you term a distant healer, it is still going through the bandwidths, the vibrations, for the only reason they can do that is because there is no separation.*

All are one.

And did we not in session 352 (The Light Traveller and The Ascension) tell you about the orange and the segments? We wish many to go back and revisit that session to learn about themselves. To learn about their many selves held together by the pith in the orange, cluster within clusters, and realms within realms.

So, yes, there are many suffering. Some that are not ready to exit can be helped by the energy healers, or by their own thoughts, by decluttering their minds. If their minds are full of dread, fear, sickness and ill health, lack of mobility, then it will be layer upon layer upon layer and that is why you get a depression. It is when something has been pushed down, depressed. And so many of these are struggling with what you term depression, for they do not see a way out, because they are looking at the same situation with the same mindset.

And we ask you this, why is it called, a mindset? Because the mind has been set. We want the mind to be unblocked, no longer set, because when something has been set in place, then there is no movement, there is no room for movement, and energy is always moving, energy is not static. That's why everything is always changing.

Should these beings wish better health, they need to look at the situation with new eyes, fresh eyes, other people's eyes. For when you are emotionally tied up within self, often you do not see the situation for what it is. So, the loved ones of these that are set in a particular mind, in order to help them to see a different way, it might be something as gentle as a massage, or some acupuncture to just introduce them to get their body moving again. Even a really warm bath, aqua aerobics – once again, water, just moving it. There are many ways to heal. Vibrational energy is going to be increasing as a healing modality. Alba, we say you are focused in the right direction for you.

A: Thanks, I have a question which does not pertain to those who are still in body. When this great leveller comes, how is it going to affect those that have not left this Earth plane that should have passed on to a different dimension but are still here, the lost souls, the spirits who haven't gone to the light? Will they be affected?

J: *All will be given the energy equally. It will help them on their way. They will be enlightened; the light will come within. Those that return, their DNA structure would have been lifted and changed to a new pattern. Those ones that chose to stay behind as you call it, it's part of their evolution and part of their plan. They were the perfect piece in this beautiful puzzle, for without them, the light-workers wouldn't have had a base to work from.*

There is no difference between those who stay behind and those that leave. It is as actors on a stage, where some leave and change into a new character, and then they come on later in the play in a different form, some say centre left, centre right, wherever they go. It is the same with all of humanity. We can't stress this enough. There are many that are listening that want to be acknowledged for the fear that they are holding for their family members.

But we said once before J.O.Y. – Just Own Yourself.

Yes, you are the mother or the father or the brother or the sister in this incarnation, and yet that person who you are so fearful for and judgemental for, in a previous incarnation which is what we call a parallel life, you were then the daughter, and they were the mother or the father, it is a cycle.

There is no wrong or right, they are but experiences. It seems that humanity as part of their emotional field likes to worry, and let us ask you the question today: how is that working for you?

A: A lot of them don't want to come back. Many light-workers are tired of their mission?

J: *You know that is their choice. What will they choose the next time around? We are showing this one Jacob's ladder with all the steps. The steps to enlightenment. And there are those that we term competitive or high achievers. They are not interested in the first three rungs. They want to get right to the top as fast as possible. There are many that choose tricky or difficult incarnations.*

Often, they take or bite off more than they can chew, and they were advised about this before incarnating into this 3D body. So, some of them, it sits heavily within them. The mission becomes too much, and they decide to exit. We hold no judgement in the Halls of Justice, for we commend their bravery and the willingness to take on courageous pathways.

There is what you term suicide on your Earth plane. We have much love for these beings. Many of them chose particularly to exit that way, in order to create a chain of events for the beings they were contracted with. There are many different ways of being, of living, and of dying, or passing over.

It is no one's job on the Earth plane, to judge another's decision to choose which way they would like to evacuate this body.

For may they not perhaps find themselves in a similar position, in a different incarnation, perhaps even in another galaxy, where they thought that what they were creating then, when they stepped into that reality, of that creation, was different to what it was when they were a lighter version of themselves?

The heavier, denser version suddenly was in what you termed, the too much basket. So, we wish all to remove judgement from each other. There is a big task ahead, but your Earth plane is magical, it is beautiful, there is much serenity, and at this stage in this transmission, Alba, when you spoke to this one about the beach today, and about seeing all the turbulence, we would like you to share that with the audience so that they understand the message.

A: Well, today I went to the beach. I had not gone in a long time because I like to be there by myself. It was a perfect day, it was a little overcast, it was drizzling, and there was nobody there. Although they had the mask-only ordinates, there was nobody there to enforce it, so I was feeling wonderful.

I took some time to meditate and enjoy the very strong breeze. Then I walked into the water which had so much seaweed. All the sand was covered in a huge layer of seaweed. I stood in the sand having that water rush over my feet, and I looked out and I said to myself, this is actually a perfect analogy as to what's going on right now.

There is so much turbulence, you could see that the ocean floor had been ripped apart. Everything was coming to the surface, littering the beaches with the aftermath of whatever storm is out there. And yet I am still enjoying the sand, I am still enjoying the beautiful sea air, with the beautiful smells, and I could just stand here and be still and just enjoy everything, and appreciate everything, even though there is turbulence.

So, it was the perfect analogy to what is happening now. It is about how you can still enjoy life, no matter what is going on out there, and you know that this is just a moment in time, and the sea will clear up again, and it will be beautiful. Everyone will come out once again, but I had that beach all to myself today, it was beautiful.

J: *Thank you, Alba. That is exactly what we wanted to remind everybody of. This beautiful incarnation that they chose, the ups and downs. This one has been meeting many people through the hypnosis sessions that she has given – giving and given. She has seen the most magnificent souls, the light coming through these beings through incredible hardships that they have had, yet they have not allowed those hardships to define them because they have risen above their situation.*

Alba, we are hopeful that through these twelve sessions on YouTube, and through the book, and through the travelling that you will do with this one, that it will help people to rise above. That it will help them to have a discourse, hold a conversation. The whole reason that we aligned you with this one for this discourse was in order to start a discourse.

We want people to start talking to each other, to start talking to their loved ones. There are many that are listening to this that are hiding in the shadows. For they are still living for others, and they are not living for themselves.

That is why we say:

For who are you living?
Why are you living?

What do you live for?
Do you not live for yourself?
Do you not live to honour the All That Is?
Do you not live to be true to self, for is that not what is called authentic, to be an authentic being?

And how many of you are sharing what you feel in your heart, about being a light being, with those you love?

What is it that you are afraid of?

Is it time to embrace self? How much longer will self reject self in order to appease another? We do not say go out and create a family war, but should someone ask, rather than be a fence-sitter, be clear, be concise, and speak your truth, for you do not know whether the other is holding, just like you are.

And we have said before, what happens to you, to your 3D, when you do not allow who you are to be. Because it mutates in your cells and a stagnation occurs. The dis-ease sets in. This is not the way, this is not the truth, this is not the light.

It is time to be the light.

A: Wonderful.

J: *For when the light, is on, so many more can see. We say it is time to shine.*

A: Great. So, I know this is the last for today but I am very curious. We started today's discourse with a meeting and a very strong rock being. What happened at this meeting? What were you talking about? Can you share that?

J: *This is about what is termed accordance. So, we are gaining accordance in the multiverses. We are gathering the galactic and the intergalactic troops, as have your light-workers, and the light army on Earth.*

So, too, do we have the beings from all the galaxies. So, we are seeing who is in accordance, who wishes to remain neutral, for all have free will. We are keeping an eye on the rogue elements, so it is a case of containing what you would term top secret, as there will be another level that would be told a slightly different version in case there will be what you term infiltration.

But where we are with the Christ light, well it is of such a high vibration that there is no infiltration at that level for we are able to read somebody, an energy being, like a book. But there are those that fall under the different rays, and so some of them have the ability to read a little less, so therefore we are sending part of our committee council to the different galaxies.

This one… did we not say in her session with you: 166 (Ambassador from the Intergalactic Federation of Light) that she is going through all the portals, for she is very social? She is visiting all the galaxies, for she is taking her blue light to the galaxies in order to align with the other blue lights to set everything in place, to get the alignment sorted so that we can keep the rogue element at bay. The rogue element is part of the universal plan. The universal plan is unfolding.

The rogue element, they too have their place, just like any of us, any being, for did we not speak earlier of judgement and non-judgement? For them, it is also cycles, cyclical. They have had their turn. Now it is our turn, but some of them, similar to your elections, Alba, in America, with the trumpet and Hillary, that election had what you call sore losers, did you not?

A: Yes, we had a lot.

J: *It is the same with the rogue element, sore losers. They do not want somebody else to have a turn. That is why there is a battle for the souls of humanity. But our tipping point is growing and growing and growing, and through the work that you do with this one and many others, the light is penetrating through the dark, and growing and growing and growing. We feel great excitement, it is as if we are getting ready for what you term the graduation party. We will see many of you back for the parade, for the celebration, we will be welcoming our family home.*

A: Sounds great, thank you. Who have we been speaking to today?

J: *Today you have been speaking with Archangel Uriel, light messenger. This transmission will spread much light and hope.*

A: Wow, thank you, what do we call this transmission today?

J: *Light-workers Unite.*

A: Sounds good, sounds like a campaign, fantastic.

J: *Well, are you not in a political campaign on Earth at the moment? We are keeping with the theme.*

A: Thank you. Anything else, or are we complete for today?

J: *Alba, we would like to thank you and all your listeners for the twelve sessions. We know that this has been a large mission. This one is most relieved that this is over. She wants the borders to open. She cannot wait to meet and greet all the other light-workers in the light army.*

With you by her side, we see much fun and many joyful times ahead. We thank you and we thank the listeners.

A: Thank you very much for that.

Our guides asked us to share this information with humanity.

In order to reach everyone we need your help. By leaving a review with Amazon or Kindle or sharing your copy with friends or family we are hopeful that a true discourse can begin so many people's voices can begin to be heard.

We feel it's time for you and all of humanity to know who you are, what you are, and how truly magnificent you are.

Wishing you much love and joy on your adventures ahead.

Jill & Alba

Made in the USA
Coppell, TX
09 August 2021